MONARCH
PRESS

New York

ℭ Career blazers®

CAREER GUIDE FOR

SALES
AND
MARKETING

by
William Lewis
and
Hal Cornelius

MONARCH
PRESS

New York

Published by MONARCH PRESS
A Division of Simon & Schuster, Inc.
Simon & Schuster Building
1230 Avenue of the Americas
New York, New York 10020

MONARCH PRESS and colophon are registered trademarks of Simon & Schuster, Inc.
Designed by Irving Perkins Associates
Manufactured in the United States of America
10 9 8 7 6 5 4 3 2

Library of Congress Catalog Card Number: 83-60308

ISBN: 0-671-47169-4

CONTENTS

v

ABOUT CAREER BLAZERS

CAREER BLAZERS, one of the most respected names in personnel placement and training, was established in 1949 and pioneered the concept of the "full service" personnel organization for people seeking job or career improvement, and for companies seeking employees. In addition to providing permanent, temporary and part-time employment opportunities for thousands of people each year, Career Blazers also offers individuals and corporations a broad range of training programs. Over the next several years, the number of such facilities both nationally and internationally will greatly increase. As noted by *Inc. Magazine*, Career Blazers has been one of the nation's most rapidly growing companies.

Over the years, Career Blazers has received countless communications from people throughout the country and in other nations seeking advice about jobs and careers. They have wanted to know how to start or improve careers, how to negotiate for better salaries, how to improve interviewing techniques and how to write effective resumes. However, most often, they've asked about the opportunities and qualifications for careers in *specific* fields. And so, as a way to respond to the queries, the idea for the Career Blazers series originated.

From the onset, it was recognized that planning or improving a career is different for each field of interest. Consequently, the titles in this series are designed to provide those who are interested with practical, productive and specific information about each represented field.

ACKNOWLEDGMENTS

For their assistance in making this book possible, the authors would like to thank the following:

- *Liz Block and Weslie Rosen, for assistance in research.*
- *John Daggan and Charles Cermele, for long hours in manuscript preparation.*
- *Susan Bishansky, for copy editing this book and others in the series.*
- *The American Management Associations, for use of their research library.*
- *The Association of MBA Executives, for research materials.*
- Sales and Marketing Management Magazine, *for research materials.*
- *The Dartnell Institute, for research materials.*
- Advertising Age *magazine and its library staff.*

INTRODUCTION

SALES and marketing have been an integral part of our economy for centuries. But it has only been in the last 100 years that sales and marketing have developed into professions in their own right. The development of an industrial society, mass production and mechanized means of transportation (cars, trucks, planes, railroads and motorized barges) created the need to sell large volumes of goods, the means to deliver them, and, thus, the means to bring consumer and seller together. The first problem the fields of sales and advertising focused on was the problem of how to sell more goods. The science of marketing was the result of the union of sales and advertising in response to the problem of how to sell more goods. Marketing focused on the consumer: What does he buy? Why does he buy? And how can he be enticed to buy more?

As the science of marketing progressed, it began to take the lead over sales. The new question has become not, "How do we sell more of the goods that we now make?" but "What goods or services should we produce and sell to return the most profit?" This transition in emphasis marked the primacy of marketing as the engine of the free market economy. In fact, marketing has progressed so much in the last 50 years—along with the development of mass communication (including print and electronic media)—that it has become a part of our economy that saturates every sector of our culture.

Who Should Read This Book

This book is for everyone who is interested in having a career that is challenging, creative, rewarding and high-paying. If you haven't thought seriously about a career in sales and marketing before, maybe you should. If you are a student, this book will show you how to prepare for a career in sales and marketing. If you are a secretary, teacher, administrator, technician or other skilled person, this book will show you how you can make the transition into the sales and marketing fields. If you are already in these fields, this book will show you how to advance within them or, by building on your expertise, how to move on to a new career.

How to Use This Book

This book is meant to be used as a resource throughout your entire career. You might want to peruse it first, skipping around to those chapters that are of particular or immediate interest to you. You do not have to read the book through from cover to cover to benefit from it. For example, if you are already in the field, you might first want to read the chapters "Advancing Your Career" and "Where Do I Go From Here?" Then you can use the "Job Finding Primer" to help you get there. If you're just beginning, we suggest you start from the beginning for the overviews of the sales and marketing fields. Once you have decided that these fields are for you, then you should use the "Job Finding Primer." If you are unsure if these fields are for you, the "Job Finding Primer" contains goal-deciding exercises that may help you clarify your objectives and skills.

CAREER
GUIDE FOR
SALES
AND
MARKETING

1

What Is Sales?

SELLING is one of the most important activities in the business world. It is the one activity that all businesses have in common—and the one that keeps them going. Almost everything, from a product to a service to an idea can be sold: bottle caps and buildings, pets and insurance, energy and communications systems—even entire companies. The range and scope of the sales field are immense. There are millions of salespeople working in hundreds of different types of sales positions. The Bureau of Labor Statistics of the United States Department of Labor estimates that there were 6,443,000 salespeople in 1978, and that by 1990 their ranks will swell to as high as 8,632,000, a growth of 33.97%, which is close to 3% above the average growth predicted for all occupations. For the year 1980, the Bureau of Labor Statistics analyzed the total population working in the sales field according to the following categories:

Occupation	Employment
Retail Trade Sales Worker	3,347,000
Cashier	1,592,000
Wholesale Trade Sales Worker	1,085,000
Store Manager	962,000
Manufacturer's Sales Worker	433,000
Insurance Sales Agent	327,000
Wholesaler	248,000

A large pharmaceutical manufacturer may employ a sales force of as many as 1,000 salespeople. There are 20 such major companies in this field and between 500 and 1,000 other smaller and mid-size companies. A specialized division of a large chemical manufacturer may employ 500 salespeople to handle its product line. The United States Department of Labor's *Dictionary of Occupational Titles* (4th ed., 1977) lists four double-column pages of sales positions, including such randomly diverse positions as sales agent, psychological tests and industrial relations; sales engineer, agricultural equipment; salesperson, sporting goods; sales representative, addressing machines; sales representative, communication equipment; sales representative, display advertising; sales representative, uniforms and sales representative, weather forecasting service. The National Sales Executives Association has a membership of 26,000 sales managers. According to the Association's membership survey, approximately 87% of the members supervise a sales force of between 25 and 500 people.

WHY SELL?

It is possible for people of any age, with any background and from most any former occupation to chart their own course in sales and realize the career goals they seek. (In deciding why you want to enter this field you may find the section on "Clarifying Your Objectives" in the "Job Finding Primer" chapter of this book helpful.)

High Income. In sales, earnings are often only limited by efforts and goals. Most people in sales cite money as their primary reason for entering the field. Salespeople earn from $10,000 a year to several hundred thousand and even more. Top salespeople can earn more than the president of their own company and many earn as much as senior executives. Most salespeople earn more than their peers who have similar backgrounds and prior experience but who have not entered sales.

Visibility. Success in sales provides a high measure of corporate visibility. Top salespeople often have access to managers of various departments and to key executives. And, since every company's existence and growth depends directly upon sales efforts, salespeople can make or break a company. As a salesperson, you may have an opportunity to learn what sells and how to sell it. You may even come up with new products or new marketing concepts based on your "hands-on" knowledge of the marketplace. Many companies like to advance salespeople into management. The highest officers of most companies, even if they have not been promoted from the ranks of the sales department, must always keep their fingers on the pulse of sales. There are some companies that are primarily sales organizations; in them, even the president is involved in selling and must be able to set an example for the rest of the corporate staff.

Flexibility. Sales work offers tremendous flexibility in terms of work location and working hours. Some sales jobs require extensive travel and others let you work at home. While many salespeople work nine-to-five, many others work on a part-time basis. This means that, more than in any other field, you can often tailor your job to your individual circumstances. With so many dual-income households these days, the flexibility of sales work is ideal for parents of small children. Many people returning to the work force also prefer flexible schedules. And, many retired people supplement their income by selling part-time.

Easy Entry and Mobility. Sales offers one of the easiest entry opportunities in any field. While many sales jobs require previous sales experience, there are equally many that can be had just on the basis of self-presentation alone, on how well the applicant can sell himself to the employer. Once in the field, sales offers tremendous mobility and transfer ability. The

basic skills of selling are similar across many different fields. Employers recognize that success for selling one product or service is a good indicator of success for selling another. If your ultimate goal is to sell a certain type of product or service, you can probably become qualified if you begin selling almost anywhere in sales, become successful at it, and then add to your qualifications by taking intermediate positions or by acquiring additional education.

More and more women are joining the ranks of top salespeople in every type of industry. The sales field seems to be one of the most popular and rewarding career paths for women. There are several national organizations for saleswomen: the National Association for Professional Saleswomen is headquartered in Sacramento, California, and the National Association of Business and Industrial Saleswomen is located in Denver, Colorado. In addition, many cities have local organizations. In the New York City area, Women in Sales has an impressive membership.

One reason for the growing participation of women in sales is that success doesn't depend largely on credentials or on a network of contacts but rather, on effort and ability. There are fewer obstacles to getting started in sales, and success can happen very quickly. Also, many women find that sales allows for the expression of assertiveness and independence.

Women are often good listeners and relate well to both men and women. These two factors are important ingredients in success. While attractiveness is often cited as a factor for the success of women in sales, there's a lot more to it than that. Being attractive may help you get a foot in the door for females or males, but the sales decision will ultimately depend upon sales ability, product knowledge, and presentation. In sales, it's performance that counts.

People returning to the job market and retirees often do very well in sales. The opportunities are more varied than in any other field, and time flexibility is a major attraction. Also, since all sales work is people-oriented, life experience counts for a great deal in sales. The more you know about people, the better you'll do in sales. Many older people have successfully re-entered the job market or started a satisfying second career by using their communication skills in sales.

Sales also offers anyone who is already working the opportunity for a second income, either on a part-time or full-time basis. Again, it's the flexibility of sales work that enables high-energy people to add to their income by selling. While insurance, real estate, and Tupperware are often thought of as typical second-income fields because they can be conveniently sold in a neighborhood or community, the second-income field is by no means limited by geographic location. Telephone sales work allows anyone, even someone with restricted mobility, to establish a customer network of any scope desired.

Many people who are not content with their current income or job can draw on their own experience to develop a second career in sales. Wherever you work now, you are surrounded by products that someone else is selling. Your knowledge of your industry might be profitably transferred to sales.

Independence. Sales can offer you a great deal of independence. Many sales positions are lightly supervised at best. If you work out of your home, for example, you won't have someone looking over your shoulder. And, even if you work out of an office, you may do most of your selling in the client's office. Self-reliance, resourcefulness and independence are some of the rewarding feelings that sales provides.

Finally, but very importantly, sales is fun; it's a *people* business. Every sales situation is a human interaction, and communication and interpersonal skills play a major role in successful sales. Many people choose sales because they like to deal with people, not with paper or bureaucracy. Part of the challenge of sales is developing a personal relationship with the client. It involves a one-on-one relationship with each client that's very different from the usual office situation. It's your job to keep meeting and winning over new people.

THE ART OF SELLING

Selling can be an extremely creative profession, and there is an art to sales. Persuading people often involves a kind of group improvisatory flair. A sales "pitch" may be given from a scripted presentation, but it is the salesperson who delivers the lines, often expanding, contracting and changing the script to fit the situation. It is a performance in which the salesperson attempts to gear his *presentation* to the responses, interests and moods of the buyer so that both buyer and seller contribute something to the development of the drama. The performance skill and intuition of the sales representative help read the interests of the buyer and find the quickest path to a sale. In the course of a sales career, the sales representative may have used the same words in similar situations thousands of times. Each time, what is said must be fresh and vital and conveyed with conviction, as though for the first time.

Another creative aspect of sales is problem solving.

The salesperson, in trying to reach the client—get the buyer interested and then capitalize on this interest—may uncover a problem of which the buyer is unaware. Often this may mean translating a buyer's problem into new terms from which it can be more easily solved, or it may mean discovering a previously undiscovered problem. The sales representative might also find a new use for his product or service, suggest modifications, and so on.

THE SCIENCE OF SELLING

In recent years, selling has developed into a science that uses the most advanced measurements, including computerized data collection systems and behavioral and psychological theory. The image of the fast-talking salesman who uses high-pressure tactics and who "shoots from the hip" is fiction. The science of sales is based on the statistics of repetitive situations. A given product is sold over and over again to an audience or "market" composed of similar groups of people having similar wants and desires. With the help of statistical analysis, sales executives can tell what sales approaches are effective in most cases. It's possible to predict with a high degree of accuracy what the buyer will be interested in, what objections are likely to arise, and what particular words or phrases will most often result in a sale.

Selling is "a numbers game." A good salesperson will make the numbers work for him. The more sales calls made, the more sales made. The more new companies called on by a sales representative, the more new accounts opened. Some sales experts believe that while it's not possible to have every company as a client, it is possible to have a particular targeted company as a client if the sales representative only makes enough calls.

Sales managers and corporate executives use the data from previous sales to predict the average number of sales calls required to close one sale and the average amount of billing expected per sale. This information may then be used to set price guidelines (and in many industries a salesperson may have some flexibility to negotiate price), establish a minimum expectation of the number of sales calls a person should make, and set targets for gross billing for each salesperson during a three-month period. Finally, these numbers may provide an objective way to evaluate and reward a salesperson's efforts.

THE SALES TRANSACTION

The United States Department of Labor's list of occupational titles in the sales field is representative of all the different kinds of sales positions that there are. But despite all the variations, salespeople have one thing in common: they sell. At the heart of selling is the sales transaction. This transaction is first and foremost a type of personal interaction in which the seller finds out what the specific buyer wants or needs. *Probing*, the discovery of needs, wants or desires, is accomplished through both listening and questioning. Of course, this probing may have been buttressed by market research, which tells the salesperson what most buyers might want—but not necessarily what this particular buyer wants. The seller then attempts to demonstrate *need satisfaction*, how the service or product for sale meets the stated needs or desires of the customer.

The way in which a product or service meets these needs is often called a *benefit*. Most benefits translate into a few basic categories: convenience, profitability or economy, savings in time, quality, morale, productivity and image (which might include status, sex appeal, peer approval, and so on). Modern sales theory emphasizes selling *benefits* rather than the product or service, based on the view that people buy not just a product or service, but what the product or service will *do* for them. A benefit is a claim that must be supported. *Features* are objective facts about a product or service that offer proof that the benefits being touted in the sale are actual. For example, in order to sell an electric hedge trimmer on the basis of its portability, convenience and mobility—of great benefit to a professional landscaper—a salesperson would point out its features—lightweight, small size, and long-lasting cordless battery pack.

Selling always takes place in a competitive environment. If a client is not buying a salesperson's product or service from another competitive vendor, then the client may be meeting the need on his own. Either way, it's helpful if the salesperson can point out an *advantage* that his product or service has—for example, the hedge trimmer may have a longer-lasting battery pack and lighter weight than a competitive product. *Feature, Advantage, Benefit* selling is often called *FAB* selling, and it is one of the more widely accepted and effective selling approaches.

As the sales representative tries to get the client to explicitly acknowledge his needs and to explicitly acknowledge the benefits of the salesperson's product or service, he is likely to encounter *objections* from the client. "It's too expensive," or "I'm fully stocked," are common objections. The salesperson might reply by sympathizing with the client and not by "objecting to the objection" and thus placing the client in an adversary position. A good reply to an objection does not counter the objection so much as it undercuts it. If the client thinks of the product as too expensive, the salesperson may attempt to show how the product will actually save the client money, or how the client will actually get more for the money than from a competing product. The sales representative might reply: "I can appreciate your concern with costs, Mr. Smith, but if I can show you how using our computer time-sharing services will actually save your company money, would you agree to try us out?" The salesperson might then use FAB techniques to prove that the service costs less than perceived, or that the client gets so much more for a little more money.

The seller attempts to maneuver the buyer through probing and FAB selling, and tries to overcome objections by moving towards a *closing question* and situation. Closing a sale is getting an order. A closing question can be asked any time during the sale, and a good sales representative will ask many closing questions from the outset and throughout the entire course of the interaction. Often the salesperson will ask *test closing* questions such as "How does that sound to you?" or "Doesn't our hedge trimmer offer the portability that you need?", in order to gauge the buyer's interest. Once the salesperson is in a closing situation he may say something like: "Would you prefer to pay by cash or check?" or "What day would be best to deliver?" or "Will you just initial the paperwork on this, Ms. Jones?" On many occasions, the expert salesperson will ask for an order without actually saying, "May I have the order, Ms. Jones?"

The buyer often tries to avoid committing to a purchase. Avoidance can be very strong, even when the buyer actually wants to make a purchase. In fact, a buyer may raise objection after objection in the hopes of being convinced to purchase once all his reasons not to buy have been overcome. The salesperson must be prepared for this, and during the sales call must maneuver the buyer into an ever-narrower space—as if herding the buyer through a maze of streets into a cul-de-sac—until the only exit is a purchase. While this adroit manipulation may seem unfair, in most cases it is effective because the buyer's objections are truly answered and because the features, advantages and benefits of the sale item are valid and the ones the client needs. People generally buy what they don't have, what they want or need. A good sales representative will control the sales transaction and nail down a sale without appearing to usurp the control of the buyer.

In most cases, the buyer will only purchase from the salesperson once a rapport has been established. The buyer may believe the sales representative's claims about the benefits of the product or service because the buyer trusts the salesperson and relies on the reputation of the company. Since a tremendous amount of selling takes place in repeat situations where one sales representative sells over and over again to the same buyer, the sales representative must be able to "deliver" what he or she sells. Otherwise, next time there will be no sale. Of course, this trust has to work both ways, too. The sales representative trusts the buyer to pay on time, not to be unreasonably difficult, and so on.

Selling is more than getting someone to pay money for a product or service. The principles of successful selling and the awareness and communications skills developed through selling may be applied to and found in all aspects of relationships. There are many people who are sales representatives without thinking of themselves as such. Anyone who is self-employed, like a writer or illustrator or computer consultant, for example, will find that his or her livelihood depends not only on how good he is at his trade, but also upon how good he is at selling himself. Selling is so much a part of our lives that its jargon has passed into common usage. "Can you sell so-and-so on that?" or "Did they buy the plan?" The "sale" may be only convincing a friend to go to the beach. Or it may, in an office situation, be getting a colleague or supervisor to agree to a revised meeting schedule. The sales goal is to gain acceptance of a certain point of view. In these personal sales situations, the individual tries to show how going to the beach or rescheduling the meeting actually squares with the other person's own needs or inclinations as well. If successful, persuasion rather than force has been at work. Selling, in short, is a way of working with others rather than against them to gain one's objectives.

2

An Overview of the Sales Profession

WHILE sales is a profession or occupation, it's not just one field like law or data processing. Sales positions can change significantly according to the field, the type of product sold, the buyer, and so on. Most sales positions fall into four basic categories: field sales, customer service sales, retail sales and telephone marketing.

FIELD SALES

In field sales, the salesperson goes in person to the customer. There are two basic ways to make an outside sales call: with a definite appointment to see the buyer and without one (often called "cold calling" or "cold canvassing"). Some sales people work exclusively by appointments while others, such as door-to-door salespeople, work exclusively without them. But most outside sales reps combine the two approaches.

When a specific time is set for a sales call, this usually means that contact was initially made by telephone either by the salesperson or by someone else in the sales organization or even by the buyer. For example, the buyer may have telephoned in response to a direct mail solicitation.

Just getting an appointment involves selling. In order to make an appointment with a prospective buyer, a sales rep must first sell the client on the idea of seeing him. This may entail describing a product or service in condensed fashion or selling the client on the benefits of listening to a presentation. A chance meeting with a casual acquaintance, old friend or previous customer may also lead to a discussion of the sales rep's product or service—and to a formal sales appointment. There are some companies that hire telephone marketing specialists whose exclusive job it is to call prospects and set up appointments for outside sales visits.

Salespeople giving presentations may use a variety of selling aids. These range from gift of gab and a sample of the merchandise or machinery to a folder or brochure, an order form, a "flip chart" presentation, and a slide show or videotape. How and when these are used depends upon the product line and/or the sales situation. Often a salesperson has a choice of different media. He might give a slide presentation to a group of people but only a brochure to sell the same product to a single buyer.

In other circumstances, especially when high-ticket office equipment or machinery is involved, the salesperson might make a team presentation with several other salespeople to several officers of a company or to a management committee. When a corporate decision is required, several calls may be needed to close the sale.

Cold calling is when a sales agent calls on a prospective customer in person without a specific appointment. The most important thing about cold calls is that they are usually not "cold" in the sense of random. While the buyer may not be expecting a salesperson, the salesperson is totally prepared to see the buyer. This means that the salesperson should know a great deal about the buyer before the call—whether the prospect is a new customer or an established account, his or her name, the times he or she is likely to be available and what his or her past buying patterns have been. The sales agent may have a good idea what the company buys and who its current suppliers are. An exception to the rule is when the salesperson sells products door-to-door to people in their homes and may only make one sales trip through an area.

Cold calling often requires cutting through various obstacles such as receptionists or secretaries who attempt to screen out visitors—often with specific instructions for salespeople. However, it's important to keep in mind that any prospect who makes purchasing decisions as a part of his job regularly receives a wide range of salespeople, and many without appointments. To the beginner, cold calling may seem overly aggressive and a bit risky. It is neither. Cold calling is both an accepted practice and a very successful one. It is a very challenging one to be sure, but it can also be a lot of fun. Cold calling is one of the mainstays of outside selling. Expert salespeople claim that *anyone* can be cold called, from the president of a company on down. If you can overcome the obstacles and learn to cold call successfully, your success in sales will be assured.

The effectiveness of cold calling lies in the fact that the sales rep can take the initiative. He doesn't have to wait for an appointment and often, just by being there, he may get to see a buyer who might otherwise have stalled the sales rep on the telephone. Also, it's often possible to get a lot of information about a company when you are actually on the premises. The salesperson is then in a position to observe all sorts of things about a firm—and the products and services it uses. And finally, cold calling can be a big time-saver, especially in a high-density urban business environment.

The Selling Process

The selling process is more than just the sales presentation and transaction, what goes on in meeting or talking with the client. The selling process also involves all those activities behind the scenes that lead up to the selling situation and that follow it. Those activities can have as critical an impact on the success of the sale as the actual sales visit.

The sales process begins with *prospecting*, which is finding sales leads. These sales leads can be gathered from many sources, such as a zip code map, a special "reverse" telephone directory organized by street address, the Yellow Pages, business directories, business publications, and especially, from compiled mailing lists. In some cases the leads or prospect lists will be provided by the company and in others, the salesperson has to research these himself. In either case, the sales representative is responsible for updating, supplementing and using the information.

Prospect accounts must be *qualified*. This process involves evaluating the likelihood of a specific prospect needing or buying your product or service and the probable volume of the purchase. A credit rating, a history of the client's payment habits, along with the ability of a company to pay for a product or service, can also be qualifying factors. Qualifying information is also used to determine the best sales strategy in selling to the client and the amount of time and effort relative to other clients that should be invested in making the sale.

Sometimes qualifying is done before prospecting, as when a pharmaceutical company keeps a mailing list of pediatricians for a new baby medicine it has developed. Sometimes qualification is done during the actual call, as when a person selling magazine subscriptions with a reverse address directory finds out that a prospect already subscribes, is moving out of town or is just plain not interested. When selling to companies, often a lot of research—i.e., telephone surveys or written questions—about the client takes place. The salesperson may learn about the prospect company's employers, annual sales, product or service mix, locations, assets and internal organization. The salesperson must also find out who the decision maker or buyer really is.

An expression of interest on the client or customer's part might help qualify a prospect. For example, anyone who calls a toll-free number or mails in a reply card for information in response to a direct mail piece, TV or magazine ad expresses an interest in buying. Qualification is an ongoing process in which all information gained from initial research and actual sales calls plays a role.

Planning and scheduling are an integral part of the sales process. First, planning for and scheduling prospecting may be done. Then, planning the best strategy for each account is determined. The salesperson must plan his calls to make the best use of time. Arranging two outside sales visits in close proximity can save a lot of travel time and thus increase sales.

Finally, follow-up sales calls must be planned. Very often sales representatives are expected to use the hours *after* work to plan and do their paperwork. Even if this is not expected, good salespeople often do their paperwork after hours in order to devote the most time available to actual selling.

The actual sales call, whether on the phone or in person, is the heart of the sales process, but not the end of it. In fact, the sales process does not even end with an actual order. The next step in the sales process is **evaluation and record keeping.** What went on in the call? Who was spoken to? What was discussed? What was learned? What can be improved? What future possibilities are there? All this information and more may be evaluated after the call and then written up in a sales report. Meticulous record keeping can be a key ingredient of success.

If the sales contact is successful, then the sale must be *fulfilled*—the product delivered or the service rendered. Often the salesperson actually delivers the product or performs the service too—as does a retail salesperson who wraps your packages or the consultant who evaluates your business. Even if this is not the case, a salesperson is often involved in fulfillment. He or she may make a call to see if delivery was made on time or that installation was done correctly.

Making sure that the customer is happy with the product or service is especially important. It is in the salesperson's best interest, and often his responsibility, to follow up on the sale and determine if everything is satisfactory. If the item sold is a product such as a computer or large photocopier, the salesperson may check on *support*—the maintenance, supplies, repair and upgrading of the equipment. The same holds true for services.

Handling complaints is part of the total sales cycle, too. Complaints *do* happen with every company; they range from misunderstandings to serious equipment malfunctions, which can cost the client thousands of dollars. When a customer has a complaint, he'll often go to the person who sold him the product, even though the salesperson may have nothing to do with the actual problem. Most modern sales training programs devote a special section to handling complaints, which is designed to provide instruction in how to "turn around" a complaint and actually get another sale. Often, the key to handling a complaint, and to having the client become more loyal to you than before the problem arose, is to solve not only the problem but to be a sympathetic listener. Here, it's the personal attention and care that can make all the difference.

Finally, the sales process ends with **billing and collection.** On a rudimentary level, the news dealer who takes your money and gives change participates in billing and collection. But even in sales where there are separate accounting and collection departments, the salesperson is often involved in the process. He must make sure that billing is timely and that special billing instructions are met. If there is a collection problem and the client isn't paying his bills in a timely fashion, the sales representative may call on the client to help solve the problem.

Consultative Selling

Consultative selling is an approach in which the salesperson looks at a holistic picture of the client's business and helps identify how, by using the product or service he's selling, certain problems could be solved, goals met, or operations improved or restructured. In so doing, the salesperson might also suggest modifications or enhancements to the product or service he represents. Consultative selling, which is closely associated with conceptual selling, was developed by people selling sophisticated products, such as computer equipment. The size and expense of this equipment means that the salesperson has to consult in detail and usually at great length with officers of a company to determine the company's needs and to advise the company on an appropriate system. The salesperson has to take into account such factors as the company's projected growth over the years, its budget, and even the attitude of its employees toward computers. In such situations, the salesperson must not only draw on his own product or service knowledge, but also on a thorough understanding of a particular company and its problems.

While consultative selling is still most often associated with more sophisticated products or services, its principles may be applied to any sales transaction. In a way, consultative selling is simply an extension of the basic task of any good salesperson—to listen and observe carefully in order to determine a customer's needs. If a relatively inexpensive item such as a tie or pair of shoes is involved, we don't necessarily use the term "consultative selling." But you can see how a problem-solving or consultative approach might be effective in *any* sales situation.

Where You Sell

Where you sell has a big impact on your day-to-day job. Where you sell means both the location of your sales "office" and where the client is. Do you work out of your home, an office or a car? You may like the feeling of going to an office every day. If you work in an office you may have little more than a desk or table top and a phone, since many companies want to encourage their sales force to be out in the field. Or you might have plush offices set up for entertaining clients and for giving group sales presentations. A typical schedule might consist of Monday in the office till noon, then out in the field till 4:30 P.M., when you come back to the office to handle calls and paperwork. Tuesday through Friday you may be out at 9:30 A.M. to start your day in the field. On Friday afternoon you may spend the time in the office planning the next week and setting up outside appointments.

Some people enjoy working at home. Many travelling salespeople use their home as "home base." And they may occasionally stop in at the business office of the company. (Using their homes as offices, they may get a tax deduction.) Some who sell Tupperware or who make phone calls for newspaper subscriptions also work from their homes. Many professional consultants and others who perform a service as well as those who sell their services use their homes as offices, too.

Where your clients are will make a big difference in what your sales position is like. Are your clients in sophisticated offices, like law firms or accounting firms? Do they sit at desks dwarfed by the open, noisy space of a factory shop floor? Or, do you visit them in *their* homes and get to see how they live?

What You Sell

Is selling the same no matter what you sell? Yes and no. In many important ways, sales is the same regardless of product or service. People are people and probing for needs, overcoming objections and the like are similar for many sales fields, but there are readily identifiable differences in the sales process depending on what is sold. These differences should be considered when you are deciding in what area of sales you'd be most effective.

The chief distinction usually made is between products and services—or products and intangibles. "Intangibles" is a more accurate term than "services" since you may be selling a concept or an idea. Many salespeople enjoy the special challenge of selling an intangible. "If you can sell something you can't touch, you can sell anything," says a sales representative for a lawyers' services company. "To create a picture in your customer's mind takes a lot of imagination." Because the salesperson doesn't have a product he or she can point to, and demonstrate on, he will have to talk about abstract concepts like benefits, advantages and features of the service. A salesperson can arrange for a demonstration of the service, but first he has to sell the client on wanting the demonstration, whether free or not. One advantage to selling a service is that

once sold, the service may continue to be provided on an ongoing basis—providing you with commission income for an indefinite period. Since many services become integral parts of the client's operations, it is often harder to be dislodged by a sales competitor.

Much of this is also true of products, however, since in a way, every product is really a service. That is, the sale of any product incorporates many services and activities—manufacture of the item, quality control, delivery, installation, repair and maintenance, billing, reorder, etc. Often when a client buys a product, he consciously buys this whole group of services as part of the package. A common example is a warranty on an automobile or appliance that guarantees service for a specified time. And when selling, the salesperson may talk about benefits, features of the product and the like in an abstract way.

An important distinction in sales is between high-volume and low-volume selling. Low cost is often associated with high volume and higher cost with lower volume. As an example, consider the differences between selling super computers—you might sell a few a year—and photocopy paper by the ream. The differences are in the cost, in the amount of knowledge required, in the length of time required to close the sale, and in the reward level, to name a few.

Another factor to consider is the length of time required to close the sale. If you generally like to see your efforts yield concrete results right away, you might be happier selling something in the low-cost, high-volume category, such as office supplies. Similarly, items like toasters or inexpensive television sets sold to banks for promotional purposes involve very heavy volume.

In contrast, sales of sophisticated computers or office telephone systems typically take time and patience. When expensive decisions about equipment are being made, many meetings may be scheduled over a period of weeks or even months, often requiring the participation of a number of people from the company. The same holds for office space leasing. Since high-level decisions are not made overnight, you might only close a handful of high-cost sales per year. But for those who can endure the delayed gratification and the suspense, the rewards can be very satisfying.

Just as the length of sales time varies with the product or service sold, so does what is demanded of the salesperson—in everything from dress to amount of research or information needed. Clearly, if you are making a sales presentation to high-level executives, your appearance and self-presentation are especially important. However, the financial rewards of selling are not necessarily commensurate with status. You can make excellent money selling anything from janitorial services to computers. Remember, lower-cost products and services can be sold in enormous volume—and the more you sell, the more you earn.

Another point to consider is that selling a highly technical product like industrial chemicals or aerospace components may be satisfying because your specialized knowledge and expertise play a big role. However, there may be a trade-off element involved in such kinds of sales. That hard-won expertise may limit your ability to move easily into other areas in sales.

Much depends also on the particular market a salesperson faces at a given moment. Is the market peaking? Levelling off? In an upturn? Are you in a growth industry? Your individual effort as a salesperson has to be weighed against general market conditions. Throughout your sales career, you will want to stay well informed about the long-term outlook for your particular industry.

How a salesperson feels about his or her product or service also plays a role. While it's desirable for a salesperson to like what he or she is selling, having a special feeling for what you are selling is *not* really necessary. A good salesperson should like the *process* of selling regardless of what is sold—as long as it's providing a gratifying level of reward.

Organization of Field Sales

At its smallest, the sales department may consist of one person—you, the sales representative. If you are not running your own business, you'll likely report directly to the owner or manager of the business. A small company can provide quick advancement potential if you are successful because so much of the business' success results from your efforts.

The sales department of a large national company may have many levels of sales staff and sales management. Bernard D. Shapiro in his book *Sales Program Management* (McGraw-Hill, New York, 1977) lists the following different layers in a national sales organization. The top level of marketing management consists of a vice president of marketing and sales. Sometimes this individual might also be called vice president of sales or there may be an additional vice president of sales. The next rung down is the top level of line sales management, and it is headed by the national sales manager, sometimes called the general sales manager. This manager is in charge of all sales force activities throughout the entire company.

Below the highest levels of sales management are the middle-level sales management positions. Among them is the national account sales manager. This manager is in charge of all sales activities to national accounts. National accounts may be special accounts where salespeople located in a central office sell to purchasers who make or influence the buying for an entire national company; for example, the national account rep for a television manufacturer may sell directly to the purchasing agent who handles all purchases for a retail chain like Sears, Roebuck. The middle level of sales management also includes a regional, divisional or zone manager. This type of manager is in charge of several sales districts, each of which is supervised by a sales manager. For example, there may be a regional manager in charge of the Northeast who oversees district sales offices in New York City; Stamford, Connecticut; and Boston. Another type of middle-level sales manager is the market sales manager. This individual manages salespeople responsible for a specific group of accounts. For example, he or she may be in charge of all the salespeople who sell to the legal industry. Such a sales manager may also have marketing responsibilities since, as the resident expert in the needs of that particular marketplace, he or she may help make marketing decisions about how to package the product or service, or how best to sell it. Finally, a company may have a product sales manager. This salesperson is in charge of all selling for a specific type of product. For example, a large company that makes many different kinds of breakfast cereals may have one individual who is in charge of all sales of a specific brand, or one product manager may be in charge of all breakfast cereals while another may be in charge of breads and cakes. This individual may also have some market responsibility as the resident expert in the selling of that particular product line, and must help make marketing decisions about packaging, distribution and selling strategies.

On the lowest level of sales management are the district or field sales managers. These individuals supervise the salespeople who go out into the field. The sales manager may have some sales responsibility of his (or her) own, he may spend his time going out with the sales force to help sell, and he may provide ongoing tips on improving sales techniques or give major presentations. The sales manager will review marketing reports, help set sales quotas in conjunction with upper management and evaluate sales performance. A good sales manager is not necessarily a top salesperson. Sales managers must also be "team players" who can supervise and coordinate the efforts of people who may be very jealous of their independence. The sales manager is also part of the administration and must be able to communicate effectively with the highest echelons of the company. For many companies, writing skills, a bachelor's degree, an MBA or similar knowledge, and previous sales experience are required for sales management positions.

Beneath the district or field sales managers are the senior sales staff, including account executives, national account salespeople, and key account sales representatives. These special salespeople handle only the most important accounts, and they may be among the most successful and respected salespeople in the entire company. Account executives ("AEs") are often found in service companies like advertising and financial services. Of course, any company can call its salespeople "account executives," and so there is no one job definition. But AEs usually are responsible for selling a service and the coordination and supervision of its delivery. AEs may, in fact, actually handle the delivery of the service itself. The national account salesperson, of course, sells to national accounts. A key account sales representative is a person who usually works in a sales office along with other salespeople, each of whom works in his or her own geographical territory. However, the territory representatives may not sell to the very largest accounts. Instead, these may be reserved for a key account salesperson.

Another type of special salesperson is called the sales engineer. This individual is a technical expert in the highly sophisticated product or service he is selling. It is on the basis of his depth of knowledge that the salesperson is able to explain the product or service to clients, answer questions and recommend any modifications to meet special client needs. A sales department is also, of course, made up of field or territory salespeople who go out selling every day within their allotted region. A large sales department may also have many administrative non-sales people, including a sales training manager who may be in charge of sales program development and maintenance, and sales trainers, who actually go out into the field and train sales staff if district managers do not assume this responsibility. Finally, there may also be sales analysts who analyze sales results, as well as assistants to sales and marketing executives, sales secretaries and various support clerks.

There are actually many different types of field sales positions. *The Dartnell Sales Manager's Handbook*, edited by Ovid Riso, distinguishes among over a dozen different types of sales representatives. These include a manufacturer's salesperson who may represent, along with perhaps a few others, the entire output of a particular manufacturing plant, or a particular type of product produced by many plants owned by the same company. These sales representatives

will usually sell their products directly to distributors or to large buyers such as Sears, Roebuck and Co. or Exxon. Another type of sales position is held by the sales agent who works for a broker or a distributor. Brokers buy from factories and sell to wholesalers or, again, to large buyers such as retail chains. One important reason why there are brokers is so that manufacturers do not need to employ a large staff of sales agents.

Another type of sales position is for the manufacturer's independent agents or representatives. These individuals are independent contractors, that is, they are self-employed. A manufacturer's agent may sell several lines for the same type of product made by several different companies. For example, an independent agent selling luggage may handle luggage from domestic luggage manufacturers as well as from a Japanese luggage manufacturer. The agent's right to represent a line may be exclusive or non-exclusive. He may, for example, face competition from other independent reps handling the same product line in the same general territory or even from sales representatives of the company that made the product he represents. There are also direct selling factory representatives, who sell products made by the factory directly to the final purchaser, usually a corporation. And, there are special representatives who may handle a specialized clientele. People who specialize in selling directly to the United States Government are one example. House-to-house (or door-to-door) sales reps sell encyclopedias, vacuum cleaners, carpet-cleaning services, cosmetics, and the like; the Fuller Brush salesperson is a famous example.

Store demonstrators sell things like pots and pans and cooking appliances in retail stores. Finally, there is the route salesperson who both makes deliveries of goods and sells them at the same time. A cigarette salesperson working for a tobacco company or a drug salesperson selling aspirin and other non-prescription drugs are good examples of route salespeople. The route salesperson may also participate in maintaining the inventory in each store, try for a wider shelf space or better shelf position for his product or product line, set up store displays and assist with special promotions for a product. Of course, it's the salesperson's job to make sure that the buyer buys as much of his product as possible. Very often the route salesperson's route will be established in advance. The salesperson thus will not go out and try to find more new buyers, but will concentrate on getting his current buyers to buy more. A route salesperson is sometimes not entitled to bonuses or commissions on sales.

Field salespeople are usually organized by territories. Territories may be as small as one office building in a large city or as large as an entire country or continent. As noted, there are other ways of organizing salespeople representing a company's product or service to keep them from stepping on each other's toes. Organization by product was one way and organization by type of market was another. A large company may integrate several of these systems. For example, a territory salesperson who handles and sells color television sets in a section of an urban business district may call on various department stores, electronic stores, hardware stores, and the like. However, he might not call on the large department stores or large hotels in his district that are part of a national chain. These national accounts may be handled by a special national account salesperson who sells directly to the client's central purchasing agent. Some products may also require special salespeople, so a company might combine territory selling, national account selling and product selling all in one sales organization.

ADVERTISING SPACE SALES

KYLE VAN SAUN, Eastern sales and marketing manager for *Runner's World and Fit*, a new magazine for women, is a sports enthusiast who has successfully combined career and personal interests. During a college internship in corporate marketing with a British subsidiary of Xerox, he realized he missed the athletic world. He had been a professional ski instructor during college and was also involved in bicycling, soccer and rock-climbing.

During college he had helped manage a ski-bike-tennis shop and, after graduating with a degree in management, he decided to go into sporting goods retailing. By borrowing from his family and obtaining a bank loan, he bought a partnership in Bromley Sport and Ski in Goshen, New York—the same shop he had worked in earlier.

"I thought this would let me wear lots of different hats," he says. "And that's the way it was—together with my partner I was responsible for inventory and accounting and personnel and, of course, for selling."

With a lot of hard work and imaginative advertising and promotion, in five years Kyle and his partner took their business from a small store to a major sporting goods outlet. They ran extensive direct mail campaigns and did a great deal of community-oriented promotion, including sponsorship of local teams.

In 1979, Kyle decided to move on. Analyzing his strengths in selling and advertising promotion, he thought of going into an ad agency but decided that advertising space sales would offer more latitude. He became a sales representative with *Air Cargo* magazine, a trade publication owned by Dun & Bradstreet.

His energy and ability was such that he was promoted to national sales manager after only three weeks.

In his current job, Kyle supervises three other people, including two recently hired junior salespeople who spend all their time on the phone selling display ads to regional and national accounts. "They're just out of school but they're doing great," Kyle says. "I hired them—one man, one woman—because they both had good verbal communication skills and excellent general intelligence, and above all they were eager to learn." He pays the junior people a salary of $10,000 as a base, plus commission. "Commissions will be the bulk of their income," he notes. "I will be very disappointed if they don't make $25,000 or $30,000 this year. In two years they should be making $45,000."

Kyle himself spends about 80% of his time on the phone, developing new business. He prospects leads from industry directories, other magazines and many other sources. Also, since his job encompasses marketing in addition to sales, he must actively develop strategies to promote sales of his magazines, as well as sell ad space.

"It's very exciting work," he says. "It's people-oriented and it offers an intelligent and articulate person the opportunity for rapid growth. If you're good, you really move."

COMMERCIAL LEASING

Just 31, ARTHUR DRAZNIN has been earning in the six figures for over three years. He recently joined Harper-Lawrence, a leading commercial real estate firm in New York, after selling his interest in Aegis Property Services Corp., a company he had formed with a friend.

"When I graduated from college, I was interested in law," he says. "So I worked for an attorney for a while but decided against law school and the profession. Then I decided to go into the business sector and considered being a stockbroker. I remember talking to one former broker who told me flatly: 'Forget the stock market. Commercial real estate.'"

When Arthur spotted an ad in *The New York Times* for "commercial real estate sales trainee," he remembered the advice of the former broker. "I took in my resume and got a job that very day at Edward S. Gordon Co., Inc. They liked me and I liked them."

Arthur had entered the high-powered field of commercial real estate, where $15 million deals are common. His job was to find companies interested in moving, locate a suitable space and negotiate a deal acceptable to both parties—the company and the prospective landlord.

Arthur did not start making big money right away. Big deals are not made every day. The first year he earned $14,000 by putting together about half a dozen deals. He did a lot of cold canvassing—knocking on doors to find companies interested in moving. By the third year he was making over $35,000 and decided to join a friend in starting Aegis.

"It was fine financially," he says. "I was making six figures from the first year. And I really found myself professionally in terms of making contacts."

He stayed at Aegis for three years before joining Harper-Lawrence. "I thought of starting my own company but realized I still had a lot to learn. I wanted to work with more experienced people."

At Harper-Lawrence, with the title of senior vice president, Arthur still does some cold canvassing but his methods are different now. Instead of going door-to-door exclusively, he'll act on reports that a certain firm is interested in moving. He also gets referrals from lawyers, accountants and previous clients. Among the companies he has represented are Wang Labs, Connecticut General Life and the Greek Mission to the United Nations.

Gil Robinov, President of Harper-Lawrence, has been in commercial leasing for 23 years. "It's a field that has changed tremendously with the boom in office construction. It's a much more aggressive business today and it's attracting a new breed of college-educated people."

Robinov prefers applicants with college degrees but is not interested in attorneys, feeling that they tend to be too inflexible. He also looks for people with sales experience, outgoing personality, strong motivation, good communication skills and attractive appearance, since business is often conducted with high-level executives. "After all, deciding to move may be the most expensive decision a company will make all year," says Robinov.

Robinov stresses that the commercial leasing field is extremely competitive. To succeed, a salesperson must be very well informed, properly trained and willing to do some very hard work.

INSURANCE

STAN LEWIS, 62, has been in insurance sales since 1950. He left his first postwar job as traffic manager with a steamship company because of a ceiling on salary. On the advice of a relative, he took a job as a salesman with Home Life Insurance. He was promoted to assistant manager and then to head of training. He then saw a growth opportunity with another firm and switched a couple more times before taking his present job as vice president of Alliance Life Associates, which handles over 10,000 commercial and personal accounts.

"The life insurance business has changed very much over the years," Mr. Lewis notes. "The old-fashioned image of the insurance salesman drawing up a deal at the kitchen table is out. Today most work is done on the phone or in the office, and life insurance is sold as a mixture of philosophy and tax law."

Mr. Lewis explained that a contemporary life insurance salesperson has to stay aware of changes in tax laws and in pension-related legislation. "Employee group benefit programs are a very important area and there's a lot of reading to do to keep up. Sometimes refresher classes are given as well."

People starting in the group benefits department of an insurance company's home office would earn about $20,000-$25,000, Mr. Lewis says, indicating a general range. In his company, they would be trained to become servicing representatives, learning claims, billing and other basic procedures. Then they would learn how to sell and to install a group benefits program. Eventually they would be assigned to an agency—a local office—of the home company. At that point, the trainee would begin to earn override—the insurance term for commission—in addition to salary.

Besides the growth of group benefit programs, other changes have had a major impact on the insurance field. One is the growing demand for term insurance as opposed to "whole life." Whole life, also known as "permanent life," involves payment of premiums and the build-up of cash values in a policy, while term insurance customers pay an annual premium for benefits only. Since term insurance is less expensive and therefore less profitable for the insurance companies, their marketing departments are now coming up with a variety of new insurance products to increase profitability.

One new product example is "Retired Lives Reserve," designed for corporate executives facing retirement. Another is "Graded Premium Life," in which premiums vary according to a certain formula. The emergence of these new products requires more of today's life insurance salesperson. "It's a highly competitive field," Mr. Lewis says. "It's always a challenge."

Mr. Lewis has had extensive experience hiring new salespeople and he suggests that a young person have a good education, preferably a college degree. "Sight unseen, I would pick a college grad over someone without the degree," he says. "Those years in college are important in helping to mature a person. Even though in person I may be very impressed by someone without a degree, it certainly helps on paper."

INFORMATION SYSTEMS: COPIERS/DUPLICATORS

When PEG TORTORA is asked why she left teaching to become a marketing representative for Xerox Corporation, her answer is simple: "Professional growth—and money."

After being extensively screened, tested and interviewed, Peg was accepted into Xerox's famous sales training program about a year and a half ago. After six weeks of training in New York, she was sent to the company's international training headquarters in

Leesburg, Virginia, for another two weeks.

"They gave us everything," she says. "The history of the company, the product line, and the sales approach." She explained that Xerox has patented its sales training and actually markets it to other companies. The particular sales approach in use at Xerox at any time, however, is exclusive to the company—and is changed or updated often to keep it exclusive. "Xerox people are very marketable if they leave the company," Peg noted. "Everyone wants to have the benefit of our training."

After completing her training, Peg began to sell office copiers and duplicators to accounts in midtown Manhattan. However, the highly competitive nature of the information services field—which also includes typewriters, word processors and laser printers, means that Xerox salespeople are constantly being retrained. "If Kodak or IBM comes out with something new, they call us into the classroom here and explain it in detail," she says. "I have to know their machines as well as I know my own."

As marketing representative, which is simply another term for salesperson, Peg works with an eight-person team. Each team member is responsible for about four national accounts and a number of "identified non-customers"—companies considered prime prospects. Peg is expected to work these leads but does not do any cold calling, which is handled elsewhere in the company.

As is typical at Xerox, Peg receives a base salary plus commission. Noting that many other companies in the information services field put salespeople on straight commission, she praises the security aspect of a base salary. She also likes Xerox's policy of incentive bonuses and generous educational benefits.

While Peg still has another four weeks of training to complete within her first two years, she is already looking ahead. The company is very advancement-oriented, she says. For example, her work is reviewed every six months and she is questioned closely about her goals. Eventually she would like to progress into sales management or sales training and hopes to qualify for a management program at that time.

FRANCHISE SALES

CHUCK LEANESS, 32, is director of franchising for International Blimpie Corporation, a chain of over 200 fast-food sandwich shops located in 15 states. Leaness, who happens to have a law degree as well as prior experience in the field of retailing, began in franchising in 1975.

"In franchise sales, you're selling a concept—a marketing concept," he points out. "For example, at Blimpie we're selling a unique no-cooking concept. We sell it as a simple operation especially suited for those without prior restaurant experience."

Franchise sales is a growth field and in the restaurant business, traditionally noted for a high failure rate, the franchise concept has special appeal. "Having an established name and logo out there helps a great deal in this kind of economy," Leaness says. "I often point to the fact that 90% of independent restaurants go under while the rate for franchised restaurants is less than 5%."

Despite this reassuring statistic, there's always a risk element and new franchisees tend to be nervous, making the franchise sales job even more challenging. "For example, many of our new Blimpie franchisees have never been in business for themselves before and now they're making a commitment of $100,000 or more. Naturally they're a little scared. Sometimes we sort of have to take them by the hand."

In addition to getting reassurance from the franchise salesperson, all new franchisees, with or without prior experience, are required to attend sessions at the chain's training school, according to Leaness, and good training is another selling point for the chain. In the training, the franchisees learn the chain's established method of handling everything from purchasing inventory to portion control.

Because a good deal of reassurance is involved in franchise sales, Leaness looks for selling or marketing experience when hiring new people. "We definitely require prior sales experience and marketing experience helps a lot. Having been in business is another plus," he says. "Most of our salespeople have college degrees but there's no firm requirement. Mainly we are looking for intelligent and aggressive people who can sell a concept."

At Blimpie the work is all on a commission basis from the beginning. Sales leads come from advertising, from franchise handbooks and from word-of-mouth. "If you've got a successful franchise concept, there's a lot of money to be made out there," Leaness says.

COSMETIC SALES

"I am very happy with my company," says British-born PAMELA WILSON, a sales director for Mary Kay Cosmetics. Pamela, 31, had previously worked in a makeup salon before she was recruited in the salon three years ago. "We do a lot of cold recruiting," she says. "That's how I got started—and that's how I've become a sales director."

In the Mary Kay organization, anyone has the opportunity to advance from consultant, the entry-level title, to sales director within six months—by recruiting a team of 24 women. The would-be director also has to prove herself in sales. One cannot become a director by recruiting only. It took Pamela just under a year to do it.

Pamela works on straight commission. She buys her inventory from Mary Kay and then sells it to customers at a recommended price. She particularly appreciates the fact that any merchandise she can't sell will be repurchased by the company at 90% of cost if she ever decided to leave the organization.

She also likes the fact that all her income comes straight from the company—not from her recruits. "We're not a pyramid-sort of organization," she stressed. "I make no money from my recruits. Anyone I bring in will receive full compensation for her sales efforts."

Both recruiting and direct sales provide important ways for a Mary Kay consultant to enhance her income. New recruits are usually found either through "cold recruiting" or by talking to women attending sales demonstrations. Pamela mentioned that almost all her recruits—and she is a champion recruiter—tend to be strangers rather than friends. Also, since being promoted to sales director, she has been listed in the Yellow Pages. She regards that listing as an important source of customers and recruits.

"I advise my recruits not to quit their other jobs right away," she says. "In my case, I was actually working at two other jobs when I started. Pretty soon I was making more with Mary Kay than I was from the other two put together. That's when I went full-time with Mary Kay."

While cold recruiting is common in Mary Kay, there is no "cold selling." All sales are done by appointment. To attract new customers, the company places "facial boxes" in beauty salons, health spas and other outlets. A woman who places her name in the box will be invited to a complimentary skin-care class or to a home demonstration of the products. There she will be taught to apply the products. 90% of her new customers are found at the beauty show (friends bring friends).

As a sales director, Pamela often leads the skin-care classes and also trains new recruits. Last year, she earned about $30,000 and expects to earn $40,000 this year.

In addition, she is eligible for many bonuses and prizes, which are awarded for meeting various recruiting and sales goals. While she has not yet won one of the famous Mary Kay pink Cadillacs, she and her team are "on pace" for a Buick Regal. The Cadillac requires team sales of $72,000 in two consecutive quarters, while the Buick requires only $48,000.

By any standards, Mary Kay is an extremely successful organization. The corporation, which is listed on the New York Stock Exchange, is also active in Europe and Japan. The company's success is often attributed to the personality and energy of the founder, Mary Kay, and to her motivation technique. "We praise people to success," says Pamela, explaining the Mary Kay philosophy. "If they fall on their face, we clap them back up again." Frequent "success meetings" are held in which a real rah-rah spirit prevails. "Everyone loves recognition," Pamela says. "That's what Mary Kay is all about."

CUSTOMER SERVICE SALES

The customer service representative ("CSR") is one of the newer types of sales positions and a very fast growing area in the sales field. A CSR is someone who deals directly with the client or customer and who, unlike most salespeople, is directly involved with the delivery of the product or service to the buyer, but seldom leaves the office to do it. The travel agent who handles your vacation or business tickets and the voice on the phone when you order clothes from a catalog house using an "800" number are just two types of CSRs. Car rental agents, theater ticket agents from Ticketron and Chargit, stockbrokers, temporary personnel service representatives, directory assistance operators, and bank account inquiry operators are just a few more examples of the hundreds of different types of customer service representatives.

The high cost and inconvenience of bringing customer and company together in person is the primary reason for the rapid growth of customer service sales. (Most estimates peg this cost at over $100 per sales visit, whether successful or not.) This growth has been made possible by developments in communications technology, from switching equipment to microwave transmission, by the "800" number and by such universal credit cards as Master Card, American Express and Visa which allow almost anyone to pick up the telephone, place an order and simply say "Charge it." Now, a company located in a small town in Wisconsin or in Maine, say, can serve the entire country with just a few operators. Moreover, the low cost of maintaining a customer service operation by telephone, as opposed to a retail store, allows customer service to be open 24 hours a day. The buying public is prompted to call and place an order with the customer service representative through a variety of mass marketing techniques, including direct mail, direct telephone solicitation, space advertising in newspapers and magazines, and radio and television advertising. There is now a greater trend towards a combination of catalog and telephone purchasing in the retail industry, where everything from computers to bath towels is sold by dialing a number. The low cost of this type of sales allows national outfits to pass their savings on to customers through discounts, which can of course make purchasing by mail or phone more attractive and can lead to increased volumes of sales.

Obviously, not every customer service representative sells. In fact, there are now two main trends in customer service—service-oriented departments and sales-oriented departments. In a service-oriented department, customer service either takes orders or supports the sales efforts of the company's sales force.

Some of these support activities include trouble-shooting, order-taking, order-tracing and order-expediting, complaint-handling, technical assisting, credit servicing, and arranging for repairs or warranty service.

Depending upon the size of the company, a customer service department may have a full staff of representatives with specialized functions; for example someone may handle taking orders, another person may handle complaints or trace lost orders, and a third person may handle credit assistance. The customer service department may be nationally centralized, regionalized or localized depending upon the economies of scale of the particular company, the type of industry and the philosophy of the corporation. A large customer service department may have operators who work in groups supervised by a customer service supervisor. A company whose customer service department operates 24 hours a day will have various shift supervisors who report to a manager of customer service. If the company has many customer service offices across the country, each branch manager of customer service may report to a national customer service manager. This manager might in fact be a vice president of the company or he might in turn report to a vice president of sales and marketing. As with the organization of a sales department, there will be individuals involved in the training of CSRs and there may be sales analysts and assistants to various managers.

Customer service positions are some of the most important positions in any company. The CSRs can be the only contact a customer has with the company, and this places the representative in a very sensitive public relations role. If there is a problem with an order, with a delivery or with the actual product or service, the CSR must act as a buffer between the company and customer and get the problem solved. In certain areas, a CSR must be knowledgeable in the technical aspects of the particular product. For example, the owner of a personal computer or software program may have a problem with its operation and need technical assistance. A technical specialist in customer service would address the problem. Similarly, an individual wishing to buy a particular software program may need technical information as to whether the software is appropriate for a given application. Again, a technical specialist in customer service would answer the question. So, even where no buying or selling actually takes place, the customer service representative may actually help "sell" the company and must be able to do things that many salespeople do—such as listen to the customer, project an air of confidence and knowledge, assess the customer's needs and project a strong, helpful, winning personality. The CSR must also have a vibrant, friendly telephone manner and excellent communication skills.

There are many types of sales-oriented customer service departments. In these departments, a CSR may do everything that his or her counterpart in a service-oriented department may do, handling complaints, tracing lost orders, dealing with credit and so on. In addition, the sales-oriented CSR will both take and solicit orders from clients. Even when just "taking orders," the CSR may actually do quite a bit of selling. The CSR may help clarify the customer's needs, suggest alternative purchases and even recommend additional purchases that tie in with the product or service initially requested by the customer. Many CSRs actually generate sales. A customer service representative may call previous customers to help reactivate prior accounts. Further, a CSR may call a list of current accounts to see if stocks are low and if reordering is needed. And, finally, a customer service representative may make "cold calls" to prospect accounts. Because of these active marketing activities, sales-oriented customer service departments are sometimes called "inside sales." Inside-sales representatives often work in tandem with outside or field sales representatives. The inside sales rep may establish telephone appointments for the outside-sales or follow up on sales calls made by outside reps to solicit or handle an order. The sales-oriented CSR has one of the most demanding of customer service jobs, and it is one of the more demanding of sales positions since it involves a mastery of sales techniques as well as expertise in the performance of the service involved.

A stockbroker is one of the most sophisticated and high-paying examples of a customer service rep. In fact, the formal job title for a broker is registered representative, since all stockbrokers must pass an examination and register with the Securities and Exchange Commission (SEC). During the working day, a stockbroker will almost never leave his or her office. The broker must constantly monitor the action of the stock market and other financial exchanges, as relayed to the broker's desk terminal. The broker's work consists of keeping established customers and new prospects informed of the market action, answering constant phone queries and quoting the current price of particular stocks, bonds, options or other investment instruments. The broker will also take, buy and sell orders and confirm the execution of those orders. When new financial instruments such as stock index futures or commodity options are introduced, the broker must be able to explain and sell the new instruments to clients. In addition, the broker must somehow find time to solicit new customers, either by following up on referrals or by cold calling.

Another type of customer service representative is a personnel service representative. Representatives call companies to solicit job orders, handle orders called in by clients and place appropriate candidates in specific jobs. Some representatives specialize in particular fields, such as law firms or temporary placement, and all reps service their assigned accounts on a continuous basis. They follow up on how their candidates are doing on the job, and keep informed about changes or growth in each company. An effective representative works closely with each company's personnel office or management to make sure that each office is fully and competently staffed. Reps will also devote time to developing new accounts by making phone calls to important prospect accounts.

HOSPITALITY INDUSTRY CUSTOMER SERVICE SALESPERSON

INA O'CONNOR is group sales director for Hilton International in the United States and Canada. She sells hotel rooms on a group basis—ten or more— to travel agents, corporations, associations and individuals. She works on straight salary and enjoys an important employee benefit—free lodging for herself and her family whenever she travels, as long as space is available.

Ina is an "inside" salesperson, working almost entirely on the phone from her office in New York. She is married and prefers not to be out on the road on a regular basis. "I do attend occasional sales meetings out of town," she says, "and sometimes they fly us up to show us a new hotel so we can get an idea of what it'll look like."

This summer, for example, she traveled to Canada's Maritime Provinces. "They wanted us to see our new Prince Edward Island Hilton. It won't even open until next year but of course I've got to book it ahead." Since major conventions often involve hundreds of hotel rooms, Ina already has booked some space as far ahead as the year 2000!

Ina got her start as a reservationist with Hilton Reservation Services back in 1968. It was her first full-time job and she says it is still a good entry-level sales position in the hospitality industry. "The job has changed but it's still a good way to get started. Then we did everything manually," she recalls. "Now everything is computerized."

Ina was promoted to supervisor and in 1974 she moved to Hilton International as sales coordinator for international hotels. The company, which is separate from Hilton Hotels, operates Vista hotels in the United States and all Hilton hotels abroad.

The hospitality industry is a growth industry and Ina likes the excitement of new hotel openings. The Vista chain, which began with one hotel in the World Trade Center, is expanding to Chicago and Washington, D.C. "It's always a challenge to sell a new hotel," Ina says. "But I love it."

RETAIL SALES

The field of retail sales employs nearly half of all the people in the United States classified by the United States Department of Labor as salesworkers. This is not surprising since most people buy most of their goods in retail stores—in clothing stores, food stores, hardware stores, stationery stores, houseware stores, variety discount stores, bookstores, and so on. Most types of retail stores fall into the following categories: small, independently owned operation usually with one location, but sometimes with several; larger regional or national chain stores such as major department stores like Macy's, discount variety stores like Woolworths or K-Mart, and general merchandising stores like Sears, in which all locations are owned by the parent company; franchise retail stores in which the franchises are bought by individuals or business groups but the rights to the trademark, special forms, procedures, equipment, and products are owned or controlled by the parent company; and, finally, manufacturers' service/demonstration retail outlets, such as the IBM computer store.

Since most retail stores are rather small, it's not surprising that approximately one in four retail store workers is either a manager or an owner. While growth from salesperson to store or department manager may be quite rapid in a small store, growth is in general limited and most small stores offer very limited benefits (no major medical or Blue Cross and Blue Shield, for example). Large department stores, national chains and manufacturers' demonstrating centers offer the greatest growth potential and usually offer the best benefits packages. However, for those who eventually wish to open their own place, working in either a small retail store or a franchise store will provide an opportunity to learn the business from the bottom up. Franchises and specialty shops are two of the important fast-growth areas in retailing. It may be that over the next decade the number of independently owned shops declines in proportion to the number of franchised or "branchised" shops. Many kinds of stores that were never franchised before are now becoming franchised, such as shoe repair stores, locksmith stores, hardware stores, even stores specializing in baking and selling chocolate-chip cookies or fast-food croissants. The personal computer/consumer electronics stores are important new kinds of outlets indicating long-term growth trends. ComputerLand and Radio Shack are franchised national chains in the personal computer/electronics field. Specialty shops like bed-and-bath shops, party-favor shops and so on are also a new trend and offer a tremendous opportunity to imaginative people who are interested in progressing from retail sales worker, to store manager or owner.

In a large retail store, an individual may begin as a store clerk, wrapper, or stock clerk, cashier or floor salesperson, and move up to become an assistant buyer, a sales or department manager and then a buyer, a store manager or a store owner. Large retail organizations also employ merchandising specialists and managers in charge of training. A retail organization with many branches may have regional or national managers in charge of various different departments or activities. For example, a large retail chain may have buyers who purchase regionally or nationally in specific areas such as bed-and-bath wear, junior wear, men's wear, and so on. A group of buyers who purchase nationally for all stores in the chain will report to a vice president in charge of buying. It is possible for a person to begin as a stock clerk, be promoted to salesperson and continue on to become vice president or even president of the retail chain. Since many large retail organizations also have customer service departments, a catalog sales office and a media advertising division, it is also possible to be promoted from a floor-sales position into the marketing area.

It is arguable whether in many cases retail selling is selling at all. A hallmark of selling is that the sales agent reaches out to the customer and initiates a sale, whether the sales agent knocks on a door or uses the phone. In retail selling, the customer comes to the sales representative. In many cases, the retail sales worker merely helps the customer with the selection and acts as cashier once the customer makes his or her selection. In these cases, it's not so much the store employee who is selling, as the customer who is buying. There are thousands of retail "sales" positions like these. And while they may provide growth potential within the retail industry or teach an individual about that industry, they are not sales positions *per se* and do not provide a solid background in sales for individuals who would like to become highly paid field sales representatives. On the other hand, there are many sales positions in which the sales agent must try and meet the customer at least halfway. He must step out from behind the counter and convert someone who

is "just looking" into someone who is buying—by using probing techniques, product knowledge and closing techniques. Stores which place an emphasis on active selling usually pay commissions. Such sales-active positions may be found in exclusive boutiques and expensive clothes stores, and in hi-fi and stereo stores and computer shops. Actually, the more the emphasis placed on actual selling, the greater the share of the sales worker's entire income will be from commissions. Commissioned sales in a retail organization is excellent preparation for entry-level work as an outside field sales representative for a company selling products or services to other companies, or even door-to-door to the general public.

TELEPHONE MARKETING

The fastest-growing area in sales is telephone marketing, and it is an area which will continue to gain in importance, as more goods and services are sold over the phone than in person. The future of telephone marketing is bright for three simple reasons: cost, control and new technology. Salespeople have always used the telephone to help in selling, almost since the telephone was invented; but even so, telephone marketing, as opposed to using the telephone in selling, is relatively new.

What is telephone marketing? It is a type of selling in which the primary vehicle for reaching the customer and closing the sale is the phone; the salesperson works exclusively over the phone and almost never sees the customer in person. However, not all telephone marketing involves closing a sale. There are three main purposes of telephone marketing: to sell goods and services, to establish appointments for outside sales representatives, and to research information when qualifying sales leads, for example. Customers "sold" by telephone marketing representatives are either corporations or individuals. Among the goods that may be sold over the telephone to companies are office supplies like paper, pens, typewriter ribbons, and paper clips. A few of the services sold to companies include personnel services, custodial or maintenance services, and credit and collection services. Executives and employees of companies may receive market research calls to find out about their attitudes towards the products or services they use. Telephone marketing to consumers involves selling such things as newspaper and magazine subscriptions, jewelry and housewares. An individual might also receive telephone marketing calls from stock or commodities brokers or from proxy solicitors. A major function of a telephone marketing department is to handle leads

purchasing, the organization of the department in which he works (if applicable) and how he is best sold. It's helpful if you can research some of this information prior to your interview (so you'll know whether the type of sales position is right for you). But, it's also good to ask questions about the buyer during the interview to help yourself better understand the buyer and to demonstrate your interest.

The profession of buying is becoming an increasingly sophisticated and important one. Advanced degrees in purchasing are taught at business schools and the purchasing department of a company may be as large as or larger than the sales department. It is not unusual for a major company to spend more than 25% of its income from sales on purchasing (as opposed to payroll or research or investments). In his excellent book on purchasing called *Purchasing: Principals and Applications* (Second Edition, Prentice-Hall, Englewood Cliffs, NJ, 1981), Stewart F. Heinritz indicates four basic areas of responsibility for purchasing agents: records management, research, procurement and materials management. Records management involves maintaining information on purchases, prices, stock levels and consumption, vendors, specifications for products, and catalogs. In order to be a knowledgeable purchaser and to provide the best materials for the company at the lowest price, a purchasing agent may have to: conduct market studies, research materials, conduct cost analyses, research supply sources, inspect vendors' plants and service facilities, develop his or her own supply sources and alternative material sources. In the area of procurement, Heinritz enumerates a number of important activities which include: checking purchase requisitions, obtaining evaluations of purchased products, choosing vendors (which may include issuing requests for proposals, called RFPs, assigning contracts or otherwise establishing criteria for vendors), scheduling purchases and delivery, meeting with salespeople, checking on legal conditions of contracts, following up on delivery, checking receipts against invoices, verifying invoices, corresponding with vendors, and making adjustments on invoices for damaged materials or undelivered goods. In addition, to complete a purchase the purchasing agent must negotiate the price. In order to get the best price for his or her company, the purchasing agent must be able to sell the sales agent on why he should sell to the company at the price which the purchasing agent wants. The purchasing agent may have to be every bit as skilled as the salesperson. Purchasing agents may also be responsible for materials management. These duties involve avoidance of overstock or stock obsolescence, standar-

dization of packaging and containers, accounting for returnable containers, maintaining minimum stock levels, maintaining inventory balance, improving inventory turnover, transferring materials and consolidating requirements.

Purchasing departments vary in size and organization. Purchasing in a company with several locations may either be centralized or decentralized. In a technical organization, all purchasing may be administrated by a director of purchasing or by a chief purchasing agent. Reporting to the purchasing agent may be an administrative assistant called an assistant purchasing agent. A purchasing engineer under the supervision of the purchasing agent's office may be in charge of developing purchasing specifications and inspecting purchased goods or services to insure that they meet specifications. Individuals who actually do the purchasing may be called purchasing agents or buyers. A company may distinguish between different levels or grades of buyers. There may be junior buyers and senior buyers, or buyers and senior buyers. Again, depending upon the type of company and its size, purchasing agents may be specialized according to the type of product or service purchased. One agent may be responsible for office supplies, another for office equipment, a third for furnishings, a fourth for office services, and so on. Companies involved in manufacturing may have a different purchasing agent for each type of raw material used in the manufacturing process, and for equipment used in manufacturing parts. Large companies may also have individuals who are in charge of purchasing or acquiring real estate, or who handle insurance purchasing and leasing.

Large companies may combine centralized and decentralized purchasing. For example, purchases of certain items up to certain amount levels may be done independently at each location. A purchasing agent may be attached to a specific manufacturing plant. Purchasing requirements and vendor selection may be done at a national level, but actual purchasing (ordering and re-ordering) may be carried out on a local level as needed. In a large national organization, buyers in a local office may report to a manager of purchasing for that office. This purchasing manager may in turn report to a regional or national purchasing manager, who in turn may report to a vice president in charge of purchasing. In addition, in the national office special purchasing agents may be in charge of the purchasing of specific product or service categories, much like the product sales manager in a sales department.

Professional purchasing offers excellent career opportunities. It is a very secure field and purchasing agents are paid a salary, not a commission on the amount of materials they purchase. So, their income does not generally swing with market conditions. A career in the purchasing of a particular type of product or service may well be an excellent choice for someone who has previously been selling that product or service. Many salespeople become purchasing agents. Similarly, people who have been purchasing may move into sales. Since many purchasing agents know each other through memberships in professional purchasing associations and through working with each other during the course of their careers, and since a purchasing agent is intimately familiar with the buying/decision process, a purchasing agent who decides to begin a selling career is at a distinct advantage over other people beginning in the same field.

BUYER

RICHARD McHUGH, associate director of corporate purchasing for ITT Corporation, has been in the purchasing field for 22 years. Today he helps set purchasing policy for the many companies in the ITT conglomerate. "Take ITT Avionics in New Jersey. They're a subsidiary of ours and they have a purchasing director who buys only for them. But their purchasing policy comes down from this office." His office also conducts major negotiating efforts on behalf of the corporation whenever any particularly sensitive buying is required. "Sensitive" buying for McHugh includes extremely high-priced goods or services, and most international purchasing. "Electronic components, for example, are now a world commodity, so our office would handle the negotiations."

Like many other people in the field of purchasing, Mr. McHugh got his start in sales—in his case, selling spare engine parts and overhauls for airplanes. "Sales is a good career path for anything. It gives a young person a lot of visibility," he says. "I was a pilot in the army and when I came out all I knew was airplanes. You could say I sort of gyrated into sales."

Then an opportunity came along in subcontracting, a branch of purchasing, and next Mr. McHugh joined ITT in a line purchasing position. "I was the guy who actually did the buying," he says. He was then promoted to department head and eventually worked his way up to his present post in the corporate buying office.

As a corporate buying officer, Mr. McHugh encourages his people to talk to all salespeople who ask. "You never know who is going to walk in here with a new hula-hoop or the best cost-reduction idea I've ever seen." But he does like to see salespeople who are prepared. "This office is besieged by salespeople who have not done their homework. A good salesperson calling on a corporate account should know that corporate account well. In any negotiation, 95% of the work occurs before anyone sits down—and it's the same in sales. If anyone's going to sell me, they better know their stuff."

SALES COMPENSATION

There are two important questions about sales compensation: "How is it structured?" and "How much can you earn?"

Sales Compensation Plans

There are six basic types of sales compensation packages: straight salary, a draw against commission, a salary plus commission, a salary plus an individual bonus, a salary plus a group bonus, and a salary plus commission plus a group or individual bonus. According to the *Sales and Marketing Management* magazine survey published in the February 22, 1982, issue, about 33.2% of the salespeople in all industries were on a salary plus bonus plan. The next most prevalent type of compensation program was salary plus commission, accounting for 29.9% of all salespeople. Straight salary accounted for 18.9%, and draw against commission accounted for 6.3%. According to a highly respected but selective biennial study of salespeople's compensation undertaken by the Dartnell Corporation of Chicago in 1981, a slightly different picture emerges. Almost 60% of the salespeople surveyed were on a combination plan of salary plus incentive. Less than a quarter surveyed received straight salary, and slightly less than one-fifth were on straight commission. This survey showed a greater share of sales reps working on straight commission. The survey included responses from over 330 companies employing over 26,000 salespeople. These companies represented 38 different industries, from aerospace to retailing.

People on straight salary receive a regular, fixed paycheck that is not tied to sales performance. However, extra effort may be rewarded. For example, some companies add incentive by offering a raise, discretionary bonuses or performance bonuses to salaried salespeople.

People selling on straight commission are paid according to their sales performance. They usually receive a percentage of total sales volume and commissions are often paid when payment is received by the salesperson's company—not when the order is placed. Commission salespeople may also be eligible for bonus payments if they exceed certain quotas. Commissions may range from 2%-4% of the gross sale in some industries, up to 50% or more in others, as in the permanent personnel business. Commissions may also be structured according to a sliding scale. For example, the sales representative may earn 5% of the first $200,000 in sales, 7% of the next $200,000 and 10% of all sales above $400,000 per year. In some cases, commissions can be based not only on gross sales, but also on gross profit. For example, if you sell a product that your company has bought from another source, you might earn commissions on the difference between what your company paid for the product and the final sale price to your client.

To tide them over until customers pay their bills, some salespeople may receive an advance or "draw" against commission. The amount of the draw is usually established at the beginning and the draw may be paid on a regular basis. However, this money comes out of the total commission a salesperson earns. For example, if the salesperson takes a weekly draw of $500 or about $2,000 a month and earns $3,000 in total commission sales for the month, he or she will be entitled to a commission payment of $1,000–$3,000 minus the draw. Some companies provide expense and entertainment accounts or budgets for sales staff. In some instances, each salesperson is allowed to spend a certain amount on travel, client lunches or gifts to clients (during the holiday season, for example). At other companies the expense may be subtracted from commissions just like the draw, or may be shared according to some formula by both company and sales rep.

If a salesperson earns less than his or her draw, what happens in each case depends on the company (and the salesperson). Some companies will carry the deficit on the books forever—or until it is made up. However, many companies will wipe the slate clear at the end of the fiscal year and give the salesperson a chance for a fresh start. Naturally, the company's decision would be based on the individual salesperson's overall performance and other factors, from adverse weather to general economic conditions. By the same token, if there seems to be no overriding reason for a continuing deficit, a salesperson may be advised to seek a new position.

Is the sky the limit in commission sales? It can be, but it depends on company policy. Some companies actually put a limit on earnings in a given time period. This would mean that even if you greatly exceeded your quota in a given month, there would be a maximum amount you could earn that month. However, in such a case, your sales manager would probably take your performance into account and either raise your base (if you are on a combination) or draw, or make other changes in the commission structure so

that you would continue to be rewarded in proportion to your efforts.

On the combination plan, salespeople receive a base salary plus commission or bonus, or other monetary reward based on performance. All sorts of different formulas are common. The commission may be based on all sales or on sales over a certain minimum or quota. The commission may be paid at a fixed rate or it may vary, getting higher as volume increases.

Under the combination plan, the base salary is just that—a salary—not to be confused with a draw against commission. In other words, if the base salary is $1,500 a month and the salesperson earns commissions of $1,000 that month, income will equal salary plus commission for a total of $2,500. The fixed portion and the variable portion may often be divided in a ratio of 70% base salary and 30% incentive—either commission or bonus or both—or the ratio may be 60/40 or 80/20.

Also, while a base salary may be viewed as the "fixed" part of the plan, it is not fixed in stone. The base itself is calculated on the basis of the salesperson's experience, ability and past performance, so as a salesperson's monthly volume increases, he or she can look forward to a higher base salary—as well as increased income from commission or bonus. However, as sales performance improves, a salesperson may also expect higher quotas.

How Much Can You Earn?

How much do salespeople make? That depends on whether they are on salary, commission or on combination plan, on whether they are experienced, semi-experienced or trainees—and on their particular industry or specific company. "In a field where sales are hard to come by—where you take a lot of risk and may only close a few sales per year—that's where the rewards are the best," says Bob Weir, a principal of Alberta Smyth Personnel Agency, Inc., a New York firm specializing in sales positions. Mr. Weir cites telecommunications, computers and equipment leasing as especially high-potential fields, where relative newcomers, if successful, can earn in the six figures within a few years. "You spend a lot of time putting together the sale or lease of a corporate jet, for example, or a new telecommunications systems for a company," he points out. "That time represents a lot of risk—and the more risk you take, the more reward."

A survey in the February 22, 1982 issue of *Sales and Marketing Management* (based on the Dartnell survey) provides the following analysis of the average earnings for salespeople for 1981:

Industry	Experienced	Semi-Experienced	Sales Trainee
Consumer Goods			
Appliances (household)	$26,500	NA	NA
Beverages	18,000	NA	NA
Cosmetics & toilet preparations	24,500	NA	NA
Drugs & medicines	26,000	$23,000	$18,500
Food products	25,900	18,756	NA
Health care products & services	31,148	24,141	20,000
Housewares	28,000	29,000	19,000
Tobacco	19,000	17,500	NA
Tools & hardware	25,000	20,135	16,865
Industrial Goods			
Automotive parts & accessories	32,300	22,000	18,000
Autos & trucks	33,000	22,000	NA
Building materials	26,500	21,750	16,000
Chemicals	31,500	24,250	17,000
Computer products & services	28,000	20,000	17,000
Electrical equipment & supplies	32,500	25,000	15,000
Electronics	31,250	27,000	18,500
Fabricated metal products	31,725	24,500	17,000
General machinery	31,000	25,000	18,000
Glass & allied products	18,500	13,000	NA
Instruments & allied products	31,650	25,116	19,600
Iron & steel	29,250	NA	NA
Non-ferrous metals	33,000	23,000	NA
Office machinery & equipment	32,000	23,000	13,000
Paper & allied products	30,000	17,000	18,100
Petroleum & petro products	30,000	NA	17,000
Printing	20,750	NA	12,000
Publishing	18,400	10,000	11,100
Rubber, plastics & leather	30,000	24,900	20,580
Textile & apparel	36,500	28,150	NA
Transportation equipment	28,300	23,000	15,500
Services			
Service industries	37,000	25,000	19,333
Transportation	30,514	25,600	NA
Utilities	30,000	NA	NA

NA = not available

Reprinted by permission from **Sales & Marketing Management Magazine**, Copyright 1982.

The Dartnell survey on sales compensation in 1981, which averaged salespeople's earnings in different industries, found that salespeople on a combination plan reported the highest average: $33,110 a year, with a middle-half annual range of $25,000-38,000. Salespeople on a commission plan did next best, averaging $32,658 in a $24,000-38,000 range. Finally, salespeople on salary averaged $29,120 in an $21,500-36,000 range. In addition, the survey found that 82% of companies pay all or part of sales force expenses apart from compensation. These figures, while slightly out of date, should offer a basic indication of potential earnings. Two important factors, inflation—which would tend to increase the earnings—and a slowdown in the economy—which would tend to reduce these figures—may work to cancel each other out.

In considering the results of either the Dartnell or the *Sales and Marketing Management* studies, remember that these must be used advisedly. Many salespeople make more, many make less—and many did not report. The Dartnell survey, for example, did not cover independent manufacturer's representatives. The Dartnell survey also found that today's salespeople have better benefits coverage than ever before, with people on salary or on the combination plan typically enjoying more benefits. An impressive 90% of companies surveyed paid all or part of medical and hospitalization insurance, 84% paid life insurance, 51% had a pension plan and 51% had a dental plan. In addition, over 57% of the companies had a tuition-refund program and 47% gave salespeople the use of a company car. "Benefits now constitute an important part of a salesperson's total income," the study concluded.

There are other ways that salespeople can enhance their income. For example, many companies have incentive programs like sales contests that reward performance either with cash, expense-paid trips, automobiles or other expensive items. The Mary Kay cosmetics company, for example, is famous for the pink Cadillacs that are awarded to sales managers who meet a certain sales quota. The Cadillac is the top prize but the company also offers many other intermediate-level incentives, such as jewelry, fur coats and titles like "Queen of Consultants" in the "Court of Personal Sales." Mary Kay is one company that has used incentives very effectively and imaginatively to motivate salespeople and to increase sales.

Choosing the Right Compensation Structure

There is no one best type of compensation struc-

ture. In many industries, all or almost all of the companies adopt the same basic type of plan and the choice then becomes one of choosing from among slightly different variations on the same theme, not one of choosing between different structures. Your basic choices are between straight salary, a draw against commission and a combination plan—the other compensation structures being variations of these. What compensation structure is right for you? The answer to this question depends upon a number of different factors, including your personality, how much you would like to earn, and the industries in which you would like to sell. If security is important to you, or if you require a steady income which does not fluctuate, then, generally speaking, a straight salary might be best. If your employer has some sort of bonus program then you will enjoy the security of a regular salary plus the knowledge that the extra sales you make could be rewarded as well. If your job also involves non-sales duties, such as customer service, then you may earn a straight salary. Similarly, selling that requires a team effort —especially where other team members are not directly involved in selling—may also be on a straight salary basis. However, if security is of utmost importance to you, then perhaps sales is not the field for you. No matter whether you're on a salary, straight commission or a combination plan, you must meet certain minimum standards for success.

On a combination plan, you are assured of some salary but you have the incentive of knowing that a significant part of your income will vary with your sales performance. The combination plan is popular since it seems to combine the best of all possible worlds. The salary aspect gives the salesperson a sense of security and the commission aspect means that sales performance is directly rewarded.

To increase motivation of salespeople on a combination plan, many companies constantly "fine tune" their compensation structure. For example, a company that wants to expand its client base may offer a "new business bonus" to encourage salespeople to step up their prospecting and bring in new customers. Or commission rates may vary with product categories, with "hard to sell" categories carrying higher rates.

As indicated above, salespeople on commission make the most money. In other words, the higher the base salary and benefits a salesperson receives, the less he or she will tend to make compared to someone on commission (given salespeople who are equally successful). That's because reward is tied to risk. "If a company cushions you with salary and benefits, that's overhead for the company and your potential will be limited accordingly. If you work on straight commission, however, that means no overhead investment for the firm in terms of salary or benefits—and more potential reward for you," says Bob Weir. But ability to go on straight commission may depend on your situation as well as on your personality. For example, young people without dependents may be able to handle the uncertainty of straight commission better than people who have to provide for their families. But selling on commission depends above all on temperament. For people who thrive on challenge, commission sales are the only way to go. And there are plenty of family men—and women—earning substantial income on straight commission.

Perhaps the most important element in sales compensation for a beginner is not how you are compensated when you have become an experienced sales representative, but how you are compensated as a trainee. For example, if you are an experienced sales representative working on commission, and you have built up a large volume of business through a diversified mix of clients, a commission income may be fairly regular from week to week or month to month. If you are just earning your stripes as a salesperson, however, you'll need some time to build up a clientele and to develop sales expertise. Some companies pay trainees a salary during the training period. Once the training period is completed, the trainees then go on a draw against commission. In exploring your first sales position, be sure to find out how long the training period lasts and how you are to be compensated. If the draw commences on the first day, be sure to find out how long it is expected to take you to pay off your draw. Salespeople working on a combination plan involving a salary and bonus or commission may not earn a salary or bonus during the training program. Once out in the field, they may be required to sell a certain minimum volume of goods and services before commissions or bonuses kick in. There are many different ways in which companies can ease the transition from trainee to experienced salesperson. Many favor the trainee by setting lower monthly volume quotas than are set for more experienced sales personnel. Find out, without expressing concern about your probability of succeeding, what the company will do for you as a trainee.

3
Breaking Into Sales

QUALIFICATIONS

There is no ideal salesperson—except the successful one. Successful salespeople come in every shape and size. People with almost every type of personality, physique, work history, education, age, life experience and special skills enter the field of sales—and thrive.

Because the field of sales is as varied as the economy, there is no one set of qualifications needed to get a start. Each different industry has its own general requirements and even within the same industry the entry-level qualifications can vary considerably. A college degree is increasingly important as a qualifier for sales positions—especially for advancement or for dealing in the service or technical areas. Many companies that view sales as a growth position, especially in the marketing or sales management areas, give preference to MBAs. While some companies have very strict entry-level requirements, often a particular company's qualifications might best be viewed as a list of "desirables"—the company would prefer a college degree, engineering experience, previous sales experience, energetic personality, and so on. However, the employer may waive one or more requirements if the job candidate has compensating strengths. An intelligent person with high energy and previous sales experience might be able to learn the technical aspects of a sophisticated electronics product on the job, even though the employer might usually hire someone with an electronics/science background. Some large companies have very intensive training programs, which last six months to one year, and are thus able to hire college graduates with almost no relevant experience or technical knowledge. But if you want to work in a technical area like medical equipment, you'll be at an advantage if you have related knowledge in medicine, hospital procedures, or the sciences.

Often, the most important element for qualification is being able to pick up the "buzz" words the client uses, and to have a basic understanding of how the product works and how it is used. Another important criterion is being able to relate well to clients. If you are selling services or products to lawyers, you don't have to be a lawyer or a legal secretary. It may be enough to dress and speak appropriately and be comfortable with them. Remember, the client first must trust you before he'll trust what you say about what you are selling.

To find out the entry-level requirements for the field you want to enter, read the help-wanted ads in the newspaper or in special industry publications. Also, call up the personnel departments of several large and small companies in the field you want to enter. Bear in mind that qualifications may vary from firm to firm.

Finally, you might call a company and ask to speak with a salesperson (as though you were interested perhaps in purchasing the company's product), and then ask the salesperson how he got his job. Keep in mind that even if you don't have all the qualifications you need for the specific job you want, it may be possible for you to qualify. For example, if you want to sell computers and the company is looking for someone with previous experience in computers, you might take another job in sales and also take an evening course in computers. Chances are that even if you don't have the in-depth knowledge the employer prefers, your initiative, sales experience and familiarity with the field from the class you are taking may sway the employer.

The Successful Sales Profile

In spite of the great diversity of qualifications, many people who are successful and who, importantly, like their jobs share some of the personal qualities discussed below. Review the list and see if you have some of these qualities. Do these qualities appeal to you? Do they seem relevant to your experience? If you can answer yes to most questions, then chances are that a sales position would be excellent for you and that you're well suited to it.

Desire to Succeed. First and foremost, all sales work requires a high level of motivation. Drive and enthusiasm are musts. People like to buy from people who like to sell and your enthusiasm is the spark that ignites the sale. To succeed, a salesperson should not be shy or reluctant about asking for the order. Selling is hard work but the potential rewards are tremendous. And the more the sales representative wants to succeed, the more he will.

Empathy. The next important quality is empathy. The dictionary defines empathy as "the capacity for experiencing another person's feelings." The key to empathy is listening ability. Contrary to the old-fashioned image of a salesman as a non-stop talker, today a good salesperson has got to be a good listener —and not just to words, but to *all* the signals that a customer gives out in the course of conversation. These include tone of voice, body language, and degree of anxiety or relaxation. The salesperson listens to what the client says about his needs so that the sales rep will be in a position to relate his product or service to those needs. And the salesperson also observes non-verbal clues to determine the customer's state of mind. The more the salesperson knows about the client, the better he sells.

Self-Confidence. Another important quality is self-confidence. The sales representative should project self-confidence and have confidence in the product or service he is selling. If he doesn't project confidence, his doubt or timidity will communicate itself—and may kill the sales opportunity. Everyone needs a little reassurance, especially when making a decision to buy, and an aura of confidence can make the difference.

Good Organization/Follow-Up. In sales, the successful salesperson takes advantage of every opportunity. His or her time is valuable and days must be carefully planned, often down to the smallest details. A salesperson must keep track of people to be called back, leads to be followed up, expense account records to be submitted. A sales position may require over an hour of paperwork per day. Good organization is essential for realizing the highest potential.

Personal Appearance. A professional image is of vital importance. People do judge on appearances and every salesperson wants to start with the advantage of making a good first impression. This is not simply a matter of putting on a business suit. Not every sales job will require business attire, but to dress professionally means to dress appropriately—and to show that you know how to package yourself with flair. Your own self-packaging, in other words, must help inspire confidence in your competence and in your professionalism.

Good Speaking Voice. While you don't have to sound like Sir Laurence Olivier, it is helpful to have a speaking voice that is clear, distinct and pleasantly modulated. And, since communication is so important in sales, it's helpful if you are able to explain concepts cleary and simply.

Spontaneity. While many sales situations will have certain similarities, no two are ever exactly alike. A good salesperson must be able to deal with the unpredictable, to handle unexpected objections and complaints. And he must be able to respond as a situation develops.

In some cases, the sales representative himself may want to create an unexpected effect. There's a lot of opportunity for creativity in sales and often a fresh approach will win over a reluctant customer.

Cool Under Fire. Sales work can be pressured work. There may be pressure coming from the boss, from clients—and from colleagues. There may be sales quotas to meet, deadlines to worry about, a sudden barrage of customer complaints. When others become upset, it is to the salesperson's advantage to remain cool. This attitude will help inspire confidence and win respect.

Dealing With Rejection. Selling is a numbers game. For every "yes" a salesperson hears, he'll get many "no's." Since every *no* may bring him closer to a *yes*, he should be able to accept rejections without taking a negative response personally, and be willing to try and try again.

CHOOSING YOUR SALES FIELD

If you decide to go into outside sales, rather than to become, say, a customer service representative or a retail store worker, you will have hundreds of different fields to choose from. How can you choose the field that's right for you? To begin, you will have to be sure that you have clarified what you wish to get out of your career, what kinds of things you like to do, what kinds of responsibilities you like to have, and so forth. To clarify your objectives, work through the process as discussed in the "Job Finding Primer" chapter. However, even after you go through this clarification process, you will most likely find that there are dozens of fields which meet your interests and abilities. While you may wish to pursue a field which is closest to your personal interests and background, it is also important to choose a field that will provide continued security and growth—especially if a high income is important to you. Even in sluggish or declining industries, like the automobile industry, for example, there continue to be many successful salespeople. A specific company, may actually grow against the declining trend and pick up business lost by its competitors who are doing less well or even going out of business. So, do not write off seeking jobs in sluggish or declining industries, but be advised that entry-level jobs may be more difficult to find, income may be proportionally lower, job security may be uncertain and mobility may be more restricted.

Generally speaking, manufacturing and heavy equipment are on the decline all across the country. This is due to rising labor costs, outmoded industrial plants, new technology and competition from foreign markets. Because of lower costs, much new construction of manufacturing plants is increasingly being done overseas. The United States Department of Labor predicts that the greatest growth over this decade will be in the service industry. In fact, the government predicts that the growth in employment in this industry over the decade may reach a high of 44% of the entire labor market. According to the Department, the five fastest-growing fields are computers, communications, coal, radio and television, and transportation. These broad categories are made up of many, many different types of industries, all with different growth potentials.

The best industry to be involved with is one in its second stage of development. That is, one that has gone beyond the infancy stage in which most companies involved in the industry are small, privately owned enterprises. As the industry begins to mature in its second stage, these companies often go public, buy each other out and consolidate or are invested in by larger companies. In addition, many new companies are formed and a mass marketplace begins to be developed with very rapid growth. During this phase there is a tremendous amount of mobility with companies entering the business, going out of the business, and changing their approach to the business. Highest earnings are usually available in this business because great growth means a lot of sales and it also means that there just aren't enough salespeople to go around. As the industry matures, salespeople who have entered the industry early are in leadership positions. They may either move up through management or become owners of businesses within the industry, or become top, solidly established salespeople. As the industry matures, rapid growth stops and the industry stabilizes. Usually in the maturing stage, a few major leaders emerge and the industry is consolidated. The weaker companies which were supported in the fast-growth stage are now shaken out. Proportionally, there may be more jobs, but growth opportunities may not be as strong and earnings may not be as high or selling as easy.

The best way to find out about the fast-track growth industries is to follow business publications for an extended period of time. *The Wall Street Journal*, *Business Week*, *Inc. Magazine*, and the business section of your local newspapers are all good starting places. In addition, the United States Department of Labor publishes monthly and annual bulletins discussing growth in various fields. Finally, if you are interested in a specific industry, follow publications specializing in that industry.

In the computer field, for example, one of the hot new areas is the personal or microcomputer. Recent years have seen the tremendous growth of companies like Apple Computer, Inc. While this industry appears to have matured quite rapidly, many predict another round of rapid growth as the personal computer, information processor and word processor all merge into one information management tool that places computing in the hands of business employees on all levels, from the executive on down to the clerk. Concomitantly, there has been and continues to be a great growth in the software field for personal computers. Many of the software companies are just now developing into national organizations and they have most of their growth ahead of them. Many predict that software for the personal computer will eventually become like razor blades for razors. There's always a need for new blades even though most people don't buy more than one razor. However, the computer and related electronics industry is not without its ups and downs. Overproduction, heightened costs of materials, new technologies and foreign competition all can have a sudden impact which can practically wipe out a segment of an industry in just a few months or years. Related to computers and electronics is the field of high technology. Robotics, the field of computer-driven industrial robots that can work on an assembly line or handle dangerous chemicals, is a field in its infancy with much promise of long-term growth. Currently, military technology—what is called "electronic warfare"—is also a major growth area. This field involves detection, counter-detection and tracking devices. In addition, cable TV hardware and wire may soon "bust loose" as cities that have selected franchizers begin to be wired.

In the service industry, information management and communications services are booming. The development of instantly accessible computerized data banks connected to each other and to the user by cable TV networks, microwave transmission, satellite broadcasting and telecommunications systems may revolutionize domestic, leisure and business life. Individuals may shop at home through a computerized video telephone, companies may communicate from computer to computer with other companies or between departments located across the street or around the world, and individuals may maintain their own personal data banks through time-sharing services. Information processing services are merging with communications systems, and an entire new industry is shaping up.

Another major new area of growth is the diversified financial services sector. Banks, brokerage houses, insurance companies and other financial services are merging into a new industry typified by the American Express purchase of a major brokerage house and a major insurance company. For banks, in particular, the growth of consumer services such as the 24-hour tellers, combination savings and checking accounts, and credit card accounts have provided tremendous growth.

Another area of projected stability and growth is the medical technology area. Medical equipment, drugs, and medical services have long been regarded as "recession proof." While medicine may not remain completely unaffected by adverse economic conditions, the long-term outlook is good —especially since the median age of the nation's population is steadily rising. Additionally, services to the rising numbers of the aged are ticketed for solid growth.

In general, services to businesses that are not dependent upon a particular type of clientele are also a good bet. The temporary personnel industry has been one of the success stories of recent years. The outlook for temporary personnel services is strong due to the high cost of maintaining permanent staff, the changeover to a service economy, and rapid expansion and contraction in various industries. But you do not need to be in a fast-track growth industry to have great career potential and job security. You can, for example, specialize in the sale of an ordinary product or service to a clientele which itself is in a fast-track area of growth. In your supporting capacity, you'll grow along with your clients.

TIPS FOR BEGINNERS

Many people just entering a field face the same catch-22: How do you get a job without experience, and how do you get the experience without a job? Fortunately, in sales, this problem is not that pronounced. To convince an employer that you have sales ability, all you may have to do is sell yourself. And so, you may have to use the same techniques a salesperson uses in qualifying, probing and closing a sale. You may try cold calling and try to get in to see a decision maker without benefit of a previous appointment. As a prospective sales representative, you'll be at liberty to use a few more aggressive tactics than might be used were you applying for a different type of position. Cold calling the sales manager is one example. Here you do not wait for an appointment, and you skirt the personnel department and go directly to the decision maker.

The main thing is to get started—anywhere you can, but the best you can get. Your first sales job will probably not be an ideal one. However, maintain a positive attitude, learn everything that you can from it, and move on when the right time comes and you have a record of success. It's helpful if your first sales job leads you towards your larger goals. So, map a path towards your larger long-term goals. On this path, be sure to include the strategies for gaining the additional education, technical knowledge and sales experience that you'll need.

There is an indirect approach to obtaining a sales

position that is useful for a beginner. This approach involves joining a company and transferring into the sales department; and it can work two ways. One way is to get a job within the sales department or in a closely related department in a non-sales capacity. Becoming a sales secretary or an administrative assistant to a sales manager or department is one of the best ways. Very often, in real-estate management firms and other service industries, the sales secretary position is directly promotable to a sales position. As a sales assistant, you will probably deal with clients over the phone, help the sales staff by making calls in their behalf, or handle calls for clients while the sales staff is out in the field. You may help do research on prospect accounts, analyze sales data, or research product information with other departments within the company to help prepare material for a salesperson's presentation. Naturally, you're also in a highly visible situation where you can get to know the decision maker, and you have the opportunity to demonstrate your verve, good organization and desire to succeed. There are many other non-sales administrative and support positions within large sales departments. For example, you could work as a clerk in support of customer service or manage records and files for a large sales staff. Also, don't overlook the possibility of temporary employment as a sales secretary or clerk within a sales department. It is another way to get your face known and to find out what goes on in the companies that you work for.

Another way to get into sales by the back door is to be transferred within your own company from a non-sales position outside the sales department into the sales department. It is best in this non-sales position if you are exposed to the manufacture or delivery of the product or service. If so, your knowledge of the product or service may help qualify you to sell it and will cut down in the cost, time and effort to train you as a salesperson.

Volunteering can also be a way of gaining experience. Many non-profit organizations such as public radio stations, hospitals, religious organizations, charitable organizations, and colleges and universities all have fund-raising drives, which may involve telephone soliciting, dinners and personal visits. Join up and demonstrate your ability to "close a sale" by obtaining a contribution. Finally, you may also want to consider taking a course in sales. For more on this, see the next chapter.

SALES TRAINEE

MARK GRAZIANO, 22, is a trainee selling point-of-sale equipment to retail outlets in Jamaica, Queens, for NCR Corporation. He joined the company soon after graduating from college with a major in business and economics and a minor in psychology.

"Point-of-sale" systems are designed for retail outlets and include anything from a simple cash register to a sophisticated computer-linked inventory control system. To insure that Mark learned the hardware, the company had him start by installing already sold equipment. "That's how I learned the hardware," he says. "You can't sell anything unless you know what it does."

It is NCR's policy to put new salespeople immediately in the field to see how they like the work. Formal training is delayed until further down the line. After about a year, Mark will be sent for at least three weeks of training.

Mark started on a straight salary of $17,200. After six months he was promoted to Sales Rep II, which means he qualifies for a bonus on anything he sells over a certain quota. The next step up is to account manager. At that point Mark will be on straight commission.

Mark spends about one-third of his time cold canvassing the bars, restaurants and motels in his territory. He does not visit units of major chains, however, such as McDonald's or Holiday Inn. These are handled by the national accounts office of NCR. "I mainly hit the little guys," Mark says. "That's where you start. I certainly would like to have some major accounts, though." To improve his chances of rapid advancement, Mark is taking advantage of company tuition benefits to pursue an MBA at night.

SOME ENTRY-LEVEL SALES POSITIONS AND THEIR REQUIREMENTS

Below is a list of entry-level positions in sales based on a survey of some of the basic industry areas. This list is meant to provide a rough idea of types of qualifications for marketing positions. Bear in mind that different companies within the same industry may have substantially different qualifications.

Industry:
Apparel
Position:
Sales Trainee; position available at entry level.
Qualifications:
—Fashion Institute of Technology graduates or a high recommendation from someone in the company. Prefer a college education but it's not mandatory. Prefer a merchandizing background.
—No experience required.
—Training program of approximately 2½ months. Trainees progress to small accounts, and to larger

accounts as their abilities permit. Generally they move to medium accounts in two years.

—Training does *not* vary depending on the product sold.

Industry:

Textiles

Position:

Sales Trainee

Qualifications:

—Must have college degree. Prefer degree from textile school, but it's not essential.

—Some sales experience is required, either during college or from summer work. The company wants its applicants to have an idea of what selling is about beforehand.

—Company is looking for an adaptable personality; someone who can work with all levels of people; someone with poise and maturity.

—Training is on the job.

—Trainees are hired on a need basis and work in the division that requires their services most. For example, today people would be most needed in dress and blouse fabric. They would be rotated to different departments, such as shirting fabrics, home sewing, promotions, home fabrics, and then back to the first department to continue their training. This inside work would take approximately 6 months and would also include showroom sales and consumer services.

Industry:

Plastics

Position:

Sales Trainee, levels 1 & 2

Qualifications:

—Prefer college degree. Do not expect a marketing degree but it's welcome, as is an MBA.

—Experience not required for sales level 1.

—People with experience would automatically begin with sales level 2.

—Looking for outgoing, gregarious people who can deal with others all day and get along with buyers and store level employees. No introverts!

—Each sales division services different markets and controls its own training.

Industry:

Canned, Cured and Frozen Foods

Position:

Sales Representative

Qualifications:

—Education not as important as experience; experience is a prerequisite to obtaining a sales position. The company produces easily identified and rec-

ognized products. The main concern is that the salesperson understands the mechanics of selling.

—Looking for a composite of personality qualities: must be ambitious and outgoing; have the ability to give and get information; understand the goals of the company. No one quality is most important —rather the overall picture.

—No formal training program.

Industry:

Drugs

Position:

Sales Representative

Qualifications:

—Require a college degree and prefer a course of technical study—in the sciences.

—Experience is not necessarily required; it depends on the position. For example, it is not necessary in pharmaceuticals.

—Evaluate candidates based on a variety of factors such as ambition, motivation, judgement.

—A person without one quality may have others that make for a desirable candidate.

—Sales training program lasts 6 months, including field work. Each division does its own training.

Industry:

Grain Mill Products

Position:

Sales Trainee, Sales Representative, Sales Analyst

Qualifications:

—College degree required; prefer business-oriented area of study.

—No experience is required but some is welcome.

—Looking for an ambitious, personable individual.

—There is a training program.

Industry:

Household Appliances

Position:

Marketing Assistant

Qualifications:

—Prefer college degree in area of marketing or business.

—College degree not essential, depending on level of experience.

—Experience not required if applicant has college degree.

—Looking for people who communicate well, are pleasantly aggressive and persistent, and who are willing to work long hours.

—Training program required of all for first 3 months. Inexperienced people could continue to train for 9-15 months.

—Training includes product knowledge, selling skills, marketing, sales promotion and advertising.

Industry:

Construction and Machinery

Position:

Sales Trainee

Qualifications:

—Require college degree. Prefer course of study in marketing or engineering.

—No experience required.

—Looking for someone who has an outgoing personality, who meets people easily.

—Training program is 18 weeks in the classroom, where there is instruction on the technical aspects of the product, and on the make-up of the company.

—After training the person spends approximately 2½ years in a divisional assignment before going into the field.

—Different divisions service different products, and training in each division varies accordingly.

Industry:

Chemicals

Position:

Sales

Qualifications:

—Require college degree; prefer emphasis in marketing and chemical engineering or chemistry.

—Experience not required.

—Seeking candidate with good communication skills who can deal with a variety of people.

—Training program lasts 9 months. Then trainee spends time with a product manager in a particular division. Trainee visits the plant to observe the manufacturing process, visits research and development to see how products are used, goes to the regional sales office, and finally goes out with experienced salespeople.

Industry:

Furniture

Position:

Sales Representative

Qualifications:

—College degree not required.

—Experience in sales is required. Applicant needs recommendation from one already in the field.

—Prefer local people.

—No training program.

—Sales reps are independent contractors and only get commission.

Industry:

Industrial, Engineering, Scientific, Mechanical

Position:

Sales Representative

Qualifications:

—No real entry-level positions. Only accept people with experience. Education irrelevant.

—Experience essential; requires a minimum of 3-5 years in high-technology selling.

—Seeking polished individual who can deal with all levels of management.

—Two-week training orientation program.

Industry:

Computers

Position:

Sales Development Specialist

Qualifications:

—No entry-level positions.

—Education not considered.

—Experience essential—must have sold computer systems a minimum of 3 years.

—Looking for people who enjoy sales.

—No training program.

4
Sales Training

THE PURPOSE OF SALES TRAINING

Unlike training for many other careers, sales training is not usually a preparation for getting a sales job. Sales training usually comes after an individual has been hired as a sales representative. In other fields, such as secretarial and computer programming, schools offer training programs for those with no experience whatsoever and then, on the strength of the training, graduate people qualified for entry-level positions. Most salespeople receive their sales training on the job, and that training is most often conducted by a sales manager. However, there are also dozens of organizations and instructional institutions that provide sales training. As a rule, these training groups do not accept self-sponsored individuals without previous sales experience—although they may be happy to take your money. Independent sales training organizations usually sell their services directly to corporations, if they are in the business of training beginners at all, and such training programs may be customized to fit the needs of a specific client. Companies that offer sales training on a generic basis open to the general public usually teach brush-up courses for experienced salespeople who wish to hone their skills, and as such they are inappropriate for the rank beginner. The main reason why there are not sales training schools

that prepare the neophyte for sales positions is that selling can only be learned by doing. Sales cannot be learned by watching, reading, or even role-playing—even though these are important elements of any sales training program. What is learned in the classroom, which should be substantial, must be consolidated and tested in the field. The sales representative must stand face-to-face with the buyer and actually close a sale by writing a real order. In sales, as the saying goes, "the proof is in the pudding." Moreover, experiences in the field must be brought back into the "classroom" for analysis and improvement. And much sales training theory and technique cannot be really understood without prior field experience.

There are a few other reasons why sales "schools" do not offer entry-level sales training courses. One is that sales is not as clear-cut a skill as typing or computer programming. Further, most companies have their own in-house training programs, however informal these may be. So, there is no need for a school that graduates entry-level salespeople.

There are many courses offered at junior and community colleges, continuing education institutions and "learning exchanges" that focus on sales and selling. Many of these courses deal with the overall theory of selling and the role of sales in relation to marketing and business in general. Very few, if any, actually teach performative sales skills. Usually, they teach the student *about* selling, not *how* to sell. However, these courses are not without value. The more one knows about the principles of selling and how selling fits into marketing and business, the better prepared one will be for a career in sales, and the more one will be able to evaluate such a career for oneself. Additionally, a concentration in sales and marketing can be a preferred major in college for sales and marketing work. Any special courses taken in the field of sales or marketing will add to your qualifications, demonstrate a commitment to sales, and may tip a hiring decision in your favor. So, if you are considering either majoring in sales and marketing in college, or taking a special sales-related course with a view towards entering the field, we encourage it—as long as you do not rely on such a course to qualify you for a sales position. You may be qualified without it.

There are some performative-based sales training programs open to self-sponsored individuals with no previous sales experience. Even though these training programs are geared to the relative beginner, it is our opinion that someone with at least a few months' experience selling will gain more benefit from them. If you are involved in selling as part of your job and if you are self-employed, for example as a consultant, then you might consider taking either a comprehensive sales training course or a number of different seminars focusing on critical sales areas, such as probing for needs, handling objections or handling closing situations. If, however, you have no previous sales experience and would like to take a practical sales training program with the idea that you will gain exposure to some basic sales skills (and you believe that this may help qualify you for a position), then you should take a sales program that is generic and not product-specific, one that is geared to entry-level sales personnel with little or no previous sales experience and that is performative—that has the student act out sales situations. The Xerox Corporation's training arm, called Xerox Learning Systems, provides an outstanding sales training program that meets these specifications. Xerox Learning Systems has many offices located in major cities and, according to at least one spokesperson, accepts self-sponsored individuals.

It has been argued that good salespeople are born, not trained. The thrust of this argument is that all a company needs to do is show a salesperson the ropes and then turn him loose; if he or she is good, then he or she will succeed. This philosophy probably accounts for the fact that many sales training programs are "sink or swim." However, this theory is incorrect. Good salespeople are trained, outstanding salespeople become outstanding through training. In other words, sales is hardly different from other professions. Training can turn most people with natural abilities into competent salespeople. Of course, there are people with an outstanding natural gift for sales. However, without the appropriate training, this gift may be thwarted and such people may be less productive than others with lesser gifts but better training. Excellent training will allow an individual's natural abilities to blossom to their fullest extent. We recommend that you give serious consideration to taking a sales training program offered by an independent training institution if you are self-employed and sell as part of your job, if your company does not offer appropriate in-house training in the areas in which you would like to improve, or if you wish to advance within your career (for example, into sales management) and your company does not offer such training, or if it would be inappropriate for you to seek it in-house.

THE ELEMENTS OF SALES TRAINING PROGRAMS

You may need to know about sales training theory and practice for two reasons. First, if you are entering the field, you will want to be able to evaluate a company's training program in order to know how it will help you succeed—especially in comparison to training offered by the employer's competitors. Second, if you are currently employed as a sales representative, you may be seeking sales training for improving your skills or, even, your qualifications if you are seeking promotion.

Sales training programs focus, in whole or in part, on three basic areas: product knowledge, client knowledge, and sales techniques. Training programs designed for newly hired sales personnel try to balance all three, giving weight to the most important area. For example, sales training for a highly technical product or complex service might place most of the emphasis on product knowledge. Such a training program might take several months or over a year, depending upon the complexity or technical depth. For a simple product, most of the training may be in sales techniques, and a program may last several days or weeks.

During the training period, the sales trainee may transfer back and forth from in-house training to field training until, upon completion of the program, the individual is assigned to his own territory. Even then, there may be more training. In fact, sales training never ends! It keeps on going because, first, no one program can possibly cover all there is to know about the product, the client or how to sell. Second, the product and market may be in constant flux. New products or product modifications may be introduced on a periodic basis. Third, sales is a performance activity, like sports or dance. So, sales techniques need to be constantly reviewed, refined and perfected —which means training. Many sales departments provide their own in-house brush-up courses in sales techniques or product information.

Product Knowledge

Before anyone can really sell a product or service, he must know what it is he is selling. Product knowledge is essential, especially in technical areas or in situations where the sales representative is likely to come up against customers who ask lots of questions— as many do, or who know many answers! Product knowledge is a broad term covering many different factors relating to the type of product or service and to the company selling it.

A sales representative should know about the *materials* from which the product is constructed. What is the product made of? How do the materials affect price or quality? What properties do these materials have? Where do the raw materials come from? How are they processed or produced? Depending upon the nature of the product, a sales representative might have to routinely answer any or all of these questions and, if the item is made up of different parts, the sales rep may also need to be able to answer the same types of questions about the parts. Further, he will usually have to know the size, weight, shape, color, durability and lifespan of the product. If the product is a mechanism, knowledge of the operation is important. This may involve both an ability to understand and explain the physical process of the operation, as well as the theoretical underpinnings. In addition, the salesperson should know how the product is used and how all the properties of materials and construction affect use. This area borders on knowledge of the client and his needs.

The sales representative must know how the product or service is supported. Is there a maintenance or service program? Where are service centers located? How long a response time is there on service? What is the procedure for obtaining parts or consumable supplies and how available are they? Of course, it's not just products that need post-delivery support. Services need it too, and the sales representative must be able to answer similar types of questions about the services he sells.

The sales representative must also know about *availability*, *quantity*, *delivery* and *shipment*. Knowledge of the company's order processing proce-

dures is a must for each sales representative. *Pricing* information can be extremely complex when there are many different products or product lines that the salesperson is handling, or when there are complex volume pricing arrangements or special financing or discounts for early payment. The salesperson may also need to know about invoicing or collections procedures.

All these different features about the product translate into *quality*. Quality is a relative term that involves a comparison and evaluation of the "components" of a product or service against the uses to which the product or service is put. Quality may also involve a comparison between competing products or services. There may be industry norms against which the product or service is measured. These norms may actually be rigidly set technical standards or specifications, and the sales rep should be familiar with these and any controversy concerning the industry standards. Quality may also involve the quality control procedures that are part of the manufacturing of the product or delivery of the service. Finally, quality also involves guarantees or warranties.

Another important element of product knowledge is knowledge about the products or services provided by *the competition*. How do they stack up against the above mentioned points against the product or service sold by the sales representative? Additionally, sales representatives should know something about *the company* for which they work—its size, its relative position in the industry, and its reputation.

Client Knowledge

The sales representative must know who he is selling to. In fact, almost everything he will need to know about the product or service he sells will be seen from the perspective of how this information will be useful to the client. Who the client is determines what his needs or wants are, and what kinds of products or services he buys. If the client is a corporation, the sales representative may need to know something about *the particular industry* or industries. He may need to know about trends, growth projections and industry leadership. The sales representative will need to know how the companies in the industries are organized. And, finally, the sales representative will need to know how the product is used by the industry and what role it plays in each industry's overall activities. The sales representative must also know something about the *individual buyer*. What is his position? How does he fit into the overall structure of the company? What are his other duties? What is the best method of contacting him? What is his psychological profile, generally speaking? Finally, the most important things a sales representative needs to know about the buyer are what he *wants* and what he *needs*. In some companies, market research may provide voluminous information on wants and needs. Knowing this information will tell the sales representative what he will have to say or do in order to close a sale.

Sales Techniques

A training program in sales techniques will focus on the following: how to prospect, how to qualify an account, how to probe for needs, how to give a presentation, how to handle objections, how to close or ask for an order, how to greet the client and break the ice at the beginning of the call, how to plan and organize for maximum effectiveness, how to manage a territory, how to expand business at existing accounts, and sales psychology, including the psychology of the client and self-motivation, and on the use of the telephone and other sales aids. Further, all this should be done, if possible, within the context of the product or service to be sold.

EVALUATING SALES TRAINING PROGRAMS

Good sales training programs are good relative to the product or service sold and the training programs offered by other companies in the field. Sales training programs usually begin with in-house or classroom training in the product or service, on the client and in basic sales techniques. After this period, which may serve as a weeding-out or qualifying process, the continuing sales trainees may "trail" or accompany a senior sales representative in the field on sales calls. Trailing may last several days, weeks or months. Or, a new sales representative may make sales presentations to clients under the guidance of the Sales Manager. There are many variations on this basic structure. Trailing is, again, a weeding-out process and the trainees who successfully complete this phase of the program, which may be either a fixed length of time or based on an evaluation, will then be assigned their own territory or group of accounts.

A word about "sink-or-swim" sales training programs. While the authors believe that the best training program comprehensively covers sales techniques in closing, handling objections, probing and the like, sink-or-swim programs are often appropriate. For example, the type of product or the client may not require an extensive training program. On the other hand, if an entire industry generally has a very "quick-and-dirty" approach to sales training, this is a good indication that either the economics of the industry do not justify a more extensive program or that the industry as a whole is not advanced—which involves no necessary correlation to how much money you can make.

Sink-or-swim training is sometimes used as a way of weeding out sales people. No one is responsible for the salesperson's success but himself. The instruction and guidance must be acted upon. So, the sales rep learns by observing, by asking questions, and by trying and failing and by trying again. There is nothing wrong with this. The person who can do it is a winner.

In order to evaluate a sales training program, a prospective employee must ask about or obtain the following information:

1. Who does the training?
2. What other duties does this individual have and how much time will he (or she) have to devote to training?
3. How long is the training process and of what elements is it composed?
4. How does evaluation of the trainee take place: are there written exams on product or client information and performative role-playing exercises?
5. Does the training in sales techniques employ role-playing and audio-visual recordings for gaining self-knowledge and improving sales techniques?
6. Are there formalized sales training materials, including manuals and visual aids? What other special equipment is used in training?
7. How much of the above discussed elements of product knowledge, client knowledge and sales techniques does the course cover?
8. How much product knowledge, client knowledge and sales techniques not covered in the sales training program is the sales representative expected to know?
9. How does the sales training program offered by this company compare with its competitors?
10. What kind of post-program follow-up is there for additional evaluation and reinforcement training?

5

All About Marketing

WHAT IS MARKETING?—THE MARKETING CONCEPT

In everyday speech, the term "marketing" is often used interchangeably with the term "sales." People often say "I'm a marketing rep" when they mean that they sell for a living. Companies often use the word "Marketing" for their sales representatives in order to give them a bit more prestige. A list of "marketing positions" might, erroneously, include positions related to sales, like stock clerk, bagger or cashier. But, in fact, sales and marketing are not the same thing. Sales—and everything that pertains to sales—is just one of the many facets of marketing.

There is no one universally accepted definition of marketing. Most people who write on marketing like to come up with their own definition of what marketing is. What makes marketing so difficult to define is that it is a variety of different corporate departments and independent companies, a series of practices and activities within these different departments and companies, and a business philosophy. Most definitions of marketing begin with the philosophy. A common thread that runs throughout these definitions is the primary importance of the consumer or buyer. It is the job of marketing to determine what the buyer needs or desires; what products or services he will buy; what will influence a favorable purchase decision; how the

product or service should be packaged; how the product or service should be distributed or delivered; how the product or service should be sold; how the product or service should be supported; and how the product or service should be priced. And then it's the job of marketing to make sure all this gets done. Marketing (in its fullest sense) coordinates all corporate operations and information insofar as these affect the consumer—and it insures that production, sales and delivery are done at a profit. As such, the marketing function is the major force in a marketing-oriented corporation. Marketing takes the lead, and operations, finance, purchasing, human resources, and research and development follow.

Of course, marketing does not play such a large role in every company. In fact, in very many companies, the development of the marketing function to the extent described is a rather late one. Many companies start out oriented around the product or service they provide. Only later may the marketing function evolve under pressure from the need to increase sales, handle competition or deal with a changing marketplace. However, many well-established corporations wishing to enter a new business area or develop a new product line will adopt a marketing approach. In certain industries, for example, like the breakfast cereals and the processed foods industries, the product is almost entirely a creation of marketing. Consumer products in general tend to be marketing intensive. In these industries the product idea is a development of the marketing function, and then the product is created and packaged around that idea—which is the essence of the marketing concept.

The "Chipwich," a chocolate-chip ice-cream sandwich, is a textbook example of the creative marketing concept at work. According to an article in *Advertising Age* (June 15, 1981), by Carmela C. Maresca and Leslie R. Wolf, the "Chipwich" was invented by a lawyer-inventor-video engineer who invested in an ice-cream shop. After unsuccessfully working with one of the largest processed food companies to get the Chipwich marketed, Mr. Richard E. LaMotta, the inventor, investigated the ice-cream industry and began on his own.

The Chipwich was a tremendous initial success and received much notice in the marketing industry. There are two elements of its success—the way the product was packaged and promoted, and the unique product distribution/sales system. What makes the Chipwich a Chipwich, and not just another ice-cream sandwich, is first of all its name. The name is fun, memorable and evocative of the chocolate-chip cookie and ice-cream sandwich combination, and it is unique (so the name could be trademarked).

Part of the genius of the Chipwich is how it is distributed and sold. The Chipwich was introduced via street corner pushcarts. Naturally, street corner pushcart business tends to be haphazard and small scale. The Chipwich people applied a market and vendor distribution concept associated with retail outlets to the chaos of the street and actually re-created the marketplace. This strategy both helped to create a distinctive image and appeal for the Chipwich (setting it apart from the competition) and to maximize and rationalize its sales.

The street carts are assigned to specific locations—just like retail stores—rather than roaming free. In this way a market area can be saturated without becoming overcrowded. The carts are restocked at their locations (just like food stores) rather than at a central location. Managers and assistant managers (equipped with beepers) circulate throughout the territories, collecting cash and coordinating restock. Unlike other street vendor systems, the Chipwich employees are selected on the basis of the image they project, their education level, and savvy. Then they are put through a training program that uses modern training techniques like videotaping. In addition, these vendors receive some profit sharing, which provides them with an impetus to actively sell the Chipwich rather than to just fill orders.

In addition to the street corner pushcarts (for spring, summer and fall), the Chipwich is sold year-round in convenient six-packs in freezer sections of grocery markets. This distribution was cleverly planned to change the Chipwich from a seasonal item into a year-round commodity. And, moreover, the ubiquitous, decorative street carts make the product highly visible and boost the sales of the product at the grocery store. The pricing of the Chipwich is also an important part of its entire marketing concept. Priced at $1, for its market introduction, the Chipwich is a competitor in the specialty ice-cream market established by Haagen-Dazs, Baskin Robbins and others. Of course, the one-dollar price usually means that no change is needed and so the Chipwich is convenient to buy. And for now it is priced high without adversely affecting sales. In fact, the Chipwich people seem to think that the $1 price is so important an asset that in an apparent attempt to increase profits, they have reduced the Chipwich size rather than increase the price.

One of the most important elements of the Chipwich is its superlative packaging—the image of the Chipwich created by the marketing concept. The sidewalk freezer carts (always kept fresh, clean and shiny) are topped with a very attractive dark rich brown, and a light creamy brown umbrella. These colors, reminiscent of the Chipwich itself (the Chipwich comes in chocolate, with chocolate chips, as well as in vanilla), are carried over to the uniforms of the vendors, to the labels and to the signs. The Chipwich company may have been one of the first to provide uniforms for its sidewalk vendors. The uniforms are delightful and help separate the Chipwich from its competitors. Carrying through the basic color scheme, the uniforms include a khaki pith helmet or safari hat, a khaki short sleeve shirt and matching shorts, and a bow tie. Together, the uniform and sidewalk cart create a cool oasis of refreshment on a hot summer day.

THE MARKETING FUNCTION

According to the marketing concept, the product is, in essence, the creation of marketing and, throughout its life—in its relation to other products made by the company and by competitors, and in its relation to the changing marketplace—the product (or service) is controlled by the marketing function. The marketing function is often analyzed according to six major functional areas: product development and management, price and cost, advertising and promotion, distribution, sales, and market research. These six categories represent ways of analytically grouping the activities of marketing and the problems handled by it, but they do not necessarily reflect how marketing departments are organized.

Product Development and Management

The product development and management function is the establishment of a guiding marketing policy for a product or line of products. It involves the development of new products, the establishment of an entire product line or product mix, and the development of a "position" for each product (how the product is placed against the competitors and what product values or benefits are presented to the public). Additionally the product development and management function involves determination of product identification, which might include a trademark, a trade name and distinctive packaging concept. In other words, product development and management gets the entire product strategy. Product policy decisions would also involve the termination or modification of any product or product line. Product design and materials specification are also two elements which come under the jurisdiction of product development and management functions. Finally, policy determination will establish how the product or service will be supported or serviced, including installation and maintenance organizations and services (in conjunction with operations and research and development), guarantees or warranties, and all information, training or documentation required by the customer to operate the product or service.

All of these product development and management activities draw upon and are interactively involved with the other five main functions.

Price and Cost

The cost and price function is an analytical and advisory one. The job of cost and price is to determine every factor involved in the cost of production, distribution, advertising and sales of a particular product or service. Based on the analysis, it is the pricing function's role to suggest profitable price levels. Of course, the actual price of a product is a policy decision and one that may be set in conjunction with marketing research and sales. Pricing schedules analyzed and recommended by the cost and pricing function might include suggested customer credit levels, volume purchasing discounts, trade-in allowances and the like. Cost and price analysis is a highly technical function and may involve specialized activities like cost-per-unit sold analyses and techniques for determining variances from planned or budgeted costs. The cost

and price analysis function is something that goes on throughout the life of a product and product line as different profit goals for a product may be set, or as different circumstances develop affecting costs, such as higher storage costs, development of new, alternative low-cost materials, or the need to replace existing manufacturing equipment. In addition to analyzing the true cost of production, and the sale and support of a particular product, a major responsibility of the cost and price analysis function is to continually evaluate ways in which the costs can be reduced—and profits can be increased.

Advertising and Promotion

The advertising and promotion function is one that is both creative and administrative. Under the guidance of the product development and management function, the advertising function administers and creates all advertising, promotion activities and public relations. Such activities include the development of ads for print, television and radio, as well as posters and billboards. The advertising campaign created in these media may be tied into direct marketing by mail or by telephone, which would again be created by advertising. In addition, advertising and promotion are responsible for point of purchase (POP) displays and advertising, and for the actual design of the product packaging. Furthermore, it is advertising's responsibility to create sales presentations, brochures and other sales aids. Many types of products and services feature sales promotion vehicles like free calendars, ashtrays or pocket calculators printed with the company name and logo. Finally, many companies run sweepstakes and contests; these too are the special province of the advertising and promotion functions.

Product Distribution

Product distribution is a planning, monitoring and coordinating function found almost exclusively in manufacturing industries—as opposed to service industries. The job of product distribution is to plan and monitor the flow of all aspects of the product from the raw material stage through the final delivery of the product to the client. The distribution function interconnects with corporate purchasing. This means dealing with warehouse facilities, inventory control, materials handling, and delivery of the product. The distribution function is also concerned with establishing the market channel system for delivery of the product to the final consumer. A marketing channel may include the establishment of a network of independent businesses participating in the chain of sale and resale. Such "middleman" businesses include distributors, wholesalers, and retailers. Distribution may also embrace the order processing function, tracing the routing of the order from the client back through all the necessary stages to the manufacturing process, or even further to the raw materials. Because warehousing, inventory management, physical distribution, and the marketing channel network system so affect the overhead cost and profitability, it is the job of the distribution function (in association with the cost and pricing function) to continually evaluate alternative and more profitable distribution methods.

Sales

The sales function, discussed in chapter 2, is part of the overall marketing function. The specific marketing activities of sales (as opposed to the pure sales activities like making presentations to clients) involve the development of sales goals, sales statistics, sales budgets and feedback from the marketplace. Sales management, specifically the development, training and organization of a sales department, is also a marketing function.

Market Research

Market research is an information-gathering function which addresses every aspect of the marketplace. The marketplace is made up of two main elements: competing products (including the company's own product line) and the buying public. Using studies, surveys, demographic statistics and various kinds of tests, the market research function answers questions posed by the product management and development function. Of course, market research itself may develop questions for study. The kinds of questions researched and answered by market research would include a definition of a particular market—who is the buyer, how much can he spend and what does he like and dislike. The market research might also answer questions about the competitive marketplace, such as what products are out there, what is the volume of sales, what is the impact of competitive markets on the company's own product, how are the competitive products priced and how do they compare with the company's own product line. It may test-market the introduction of a new product or, based on information-gathering procedures, forecast the potential of a specific product or brand. The market research function, which is built on a combination of statistical analysis psychology and empirical procedures, is a quasi-scientific underpinning of the field of marketing. While market research does not ensure that the marketing and sales efforts will be successful, it does help the marketing manager understand what

is most likely to be successful, and why something is or isn't successful.

ORGANIZATION OF THE MARKETING FUNCTION

The six major marketing functions are organized in many different ways. The most basic distinction among the various methods of organizing the overall marketing function is between in-house corporate marketing departments and special marketing companies providing marketing services like advertising, public relations or marketing research to manufacturers and service companies. A particular manufacturing company may handle almost all its marketing functions in-house, or it may delegate almost all of them to an outside service company. Few established companies delegate all their marketing to independent service organizations and few of even the largest companies handle all their own marketing. The general practice is to delegate, to a lesser or greater degree, some portion of marketing to outside marketing services.

In-House Marketing Departments

There are five basic methods of organizing the marketing function within a manufacturing or service company. They are: function, brand, market or consumer, market channel/distribution system, and region. In actual practice companies may combine one or more basic methods to produce hybrid variants. There is no one standard practice even for companies of the same size within the same industry—although size, product and type of market do play influential roles in determining how the marketing function of a given company is organized. In-house marketing departments of smaller companies may be adjuncts of the sales department, and the coordination of all marketing functions may be handled by the sales manager and the corporate executives. As the need for marketing in such a company expands, a marketing manager may be appointed who will then administer and coordinate this expanded function. The duties of such a marketing manager, very often a vice president, are usually to supervise the sales force, including the sales manager, and to coordinate the use of outside marketing services, while setting policy with the senior administration of the company.

As the marketing manager hires additional staff, he or she may organize the staff functionally. In a fully developed marketing department there may be separate departments or sections for each major function: product development and management, cost and pricing, advertising and promotion, product distribution, sales. These departments, each headed by a department manager, may in turn be subdivided into complete departments or sections in themselves. For example, a company might have within the advertising department a direct marketing section (for direct mail and telephone marketing), a print media section and a packaging section.

There may not be, in every functionally organized company, a separate department for each function. Sometimes the functions are absorbed by other departments. For example, distribution and cost analysis functions may be divided between operations (a non-marketing department) and sales. Of course, in a functional department, many activities will be delegated to outside marketing services. Generally speaking, policy and administrative functions are retained within house, and creative or technical/analytical functions are delegated to outside services. For this reason the creative aspects of advertising are usually delegated to advertising agencies. In working with an advertising agency, a vice president of marketing and a marketing manager may tell the agency what they wish the agency to accomplish. The agency then may come up with all the creative work connected with the advertising, including graphics and copy.

Functional marketing departments may be organized into two main wings in order to facilitate management of larger departments. The two wings are first an operations group, headed by a manager, which includes advertising, sales and distribution, and second, a staff group, which includes product development, costs and price, and market research.

Brand management is the second of the two most popular methods of marketing organization. In brand management organizations, each brand or brand group may have its own specialized functional subsections. For example, a major food company might have a breakfast cereals group and a baked-goods group, each group being composed of several different brands. Each brand group or brand may have its own advertising department, distribution department, sales force, and product development and management group all working under one brand group manager. In this particular example, costs and pricing, and marketing functions may be organized in separate departments serving all brand groups alike. However, a particular brand group may perform some of its own market research functions, or all market research may be handled by an outside service.

A manufacturing or service company with one or more basically similar product lines selling to a variety of different types of buyers might be organized accord-

ing to the various different markets it serves. Some of the different types of markets may be the individual consumer, businesses, industrial companies, or local, state and federal governmental agencies. Each distinct market might require a completely different marketing campaign, different packaging of same or similar products, and different market channel systems. So, such a company might be organized by Market Divisions in which each is supervised by a manager who may draw upon support from various functional departments, or supervise his own functional department serving only his market. In another company, the marketing department may be organized according to the various industries served; for example, there may be a marketing manager in charge of the legal market, and another in charge of banking, and a third in charge of retail organizations. Here each market group may have its own sales force, advertising department and product line.

Companies that are organized regionally are usually decentralized. In such cases, a small central office coordinates the national or international regions. Each region will be supervised by a regional manager who handles marketing, advertising, sales and distribution within his territory. Marketing research may be handled by the national headquarters, within the regional division or by an outside service. Companies may opt for regional organizations when they are very large or when the regional markets are extremely divergent. For example, marketing a consumer item in different parts of the country or in different countries might necessitate different marketing strategies.

Finally, an in-house marketing department may be organized according to the different kinds of marketing channel systems used to deliver the product. For example, a company that both sells its product directly to the customer through direct mail or telephone selling, and that also sells its product to distributors, may divide its marketing department into two basic sections: a direct sales section and a distributor sales section.

Marketing Service Organizations

How in-house corporate marketing departments are organized is only half the story in the field of marketing. The great variety and number of marketing service organizations make up the rest. The most common types of service organizations are: advertising, public relations, sales promotion and market research. There are, in addition, a host of miscellaneous specialized companies and individual consultants providing marketing services. Advertising agencies are the largest and most well-known of the marketing service firms. Many advertising agencies also perform activities like market research or public relations. The two main pillars of advertising agencies are creative services and account services/management. The creative group is the group of copywriters, artists and designers who dream up and execute all the ads, commercials, brochures and collateral materials. The account services or management group is the business end of the advertising agency. This group goes out and opens up new corporate accounts and coordinates and manages all advertising agency services for the client. Serving these two main foundations of the advertising agency business are a variety of support departments. The production department coordinates the development of the advertising product from creation through delivery of the finished work. It must insure that each step along the way is done correctly and on schedule. The traffic department monitors the physical flow of layouts, photos, copy and the like both within the agency and without, as these are sent back and forth to various specialty houses. For example, the traffic department may tell the account services or production groups that a specific item like a layout has been sent to an outside photostat house for reproduction. The media buying group purchases advertising space in magazines and newspapers, and airtime on radio and TV. This is an extremely important function since most advertising agencies earn a large part of their income through commissions on purchased space. Usually, the media company—the newspaper or radio station—will refund to the advertising agency fifteen percent of the purchase price of the space or airtime paid for by the agency's corporate client. However, agencies also charge for creative services like market research or the development of a brochure. A function closely associated with media buying is media research. The function of media research is to insure that the corporate client gets the most for the money when buying advertising space. For example, a company selling personal computers must decide how best to spend its advertising budget. Should it advertise primarily in national magazines like *Business Week* or *Time*? How much advertising space should it spend on television, and how much in special computer magazines like *Creative Computing*. An advertising agency might also have a marketing research department and a public relations department.

How these basic sections of an advertising agency are organized into specific departments or work with each other depends upon the size, type, and philosophy of the particular agency. Most agencies develop teams of account executive and creative people working together on a specific product or for a specific client. In agencies with larger accounts, a specific team might spend its entire career within the agency working on just one account or product. While in other agencies, account executives might each have several different accounts, and specific creative people might work with several different account executives.

Marketing research firms make up the next major service group. Often called "suppliers," market research firms may be full service (they do almost everything in the field), or specialized in one or more areas, such as interviewing, statistical analysis, product testing or demographic analysis. For example, a specific company might have computerized the results of the United States Census and can provide that information to advertising agencies or corporations who, say, want to know how many people between the ages of 18 and 36 earn over $20,000 per year and live within a given area. Other companies may just interview people over the phone or in person. Auditing companies verify the paid circulation of newspapers and magazines, or count the number of people watching or listening to TV or radio programs. Other companies check newspapers, magazines, radio shows and television programs to make sure that the ads that were supposed to appear, did appear at the appropriate time.

The basic areas within a marketing research organization are project coordination, which involves the formulation of marketing research proposals and the specification of the methodologies to be employed; research, which involves the collection of data from archival sources; field research, which involves conducting surveys and tests of actual or potential consumers; and statistical analysis, which involves the tabulation and analysis of market research results. (For more information on market research services, check the section "For Further Reading" on directories and associations in market research at the end of the book.)

The public relations service companies attempt to get "free" publicity for their clients in order to directly or indirectly increase sales or improve the company's image (which, of course, may help indirectly increase sales). Based on the client's objectives, the public relations firm must come up with a public relations campaign that meets these objectives. Once the basic idea has been developed—this idea might be developed by the client, the client's advertising agency or the public relations firm—then it must be packaged and presented to the press. Public relations firms work by trying to get the general press, a trade press, or radio or television news stations to do a story that features the company or its product. For example, the public relations firm may send out a press release to a variety of general and business publications announcing a new product. In order to increase the likelihood of a feature story on the new product introduction, the public relations firm must come up with a "story angle" that will be of interest to the readers of a publication. Or, in order to improve the public image of a company, the public relations firm might decide that donating money to a charity would be an ideal way to gain the attention of the press and the favor of the public. In public relations firms, there are usually account executives and creative people. In addition, there is usually a media list management department or research department that maintains the names, addresses and other contact information on editors of publications, according to their editorial function, type of publication and the audience involved. There are specific companies that just handle mailing list management and mailing functions for public relations firms and in-house public relations departments.

Finally, sales promotion companies specialize in handling promotion items like giveaways, tournaments or contests to help increase sales. For example, a pharmaceutical manufacturing company may go to a sales promotion company for an item that will help boost the sales of its prescription drugs. The sales promotion firm might come up with a desk-top prescription pad holder and pen set that has both the name of the physician and of the pharmaceutical company engraved on it. The creativity in sales promotion involves both creating the basic idea for the sales promotion item and then designing it. Of course, the promotion item must be available in the quantity and at the price that will make the promotion cost-effective. There are specific companies that just specialize in finding or furnishing items to be used for sales promotions. Sales promotion companies may have account executives, designers and copy editors. If the sales promotion company specializes in an area like contests, it may also have a list management service for sending contest entry forms in the mail.

POSITIONS IN MARKETING

Every function in marketing is either administrative or managerial, creative, technical or analytical, or clerical/support. Each of the narrowest of functions discussed in the overview above can form the basis of an entire job in the field of marketing. For example, an individual working in a corporate marketing department may spend all of his or her time compiling sales statistics on the performance of a specific product according to market region or type of retail outlet, and comparing these statistics against unsold inventories. Of course, any given position in the field of marketing may combine a number of different, only loosely related marketing functions. From a corporate point of view, marketing is primarily an administrative or managerial function. Management here does not necessarily mean supervising other personnel; it usually means coordinating with other corporate departments (including both marketing departments and operation departments), as well as with outside services. Each major marketing function will have someone who is in charge of managing that function, whether or not there is a specific internal department to handle the performance of that function. Creative, technical or analytical, or clerical or support positions within marketing are usually stepping-stones to the management positions. In many cases, companies will teach its future marketing managers the business by starting them in a support capacity.

The primary positions in marketing are in marketing management—the marketing manager or vice president of marketing—and more specifically in product development or management. Positions here are brand manager, group brand manager and new product manager. Reporting to these managers may be, in a brand-oriented company, various subsidiary managers including an advertising manager, a sales manager, a customer service manager, and a packaging manager. Reporting to each of these managers may be various assistants, often called assistant or associate brand managers or managers of the specific functions. In the advertising department there may be a manager of media buying, and a manager of creative services who coordinates creative services in the areas of packaging, art, photography and print production. A specific company may have a manager of distributor relations who develops and implements the policy towards distributors for the company, which may involve working with the sales department or establishing authorized distributor programs. In marketing research there is usually a director of marketing research, and there may be several different levels of project directors. Of course, that is just the project direction side of market research. There may also be a manager of field services who is charge of coordinating all the market research teams. In the market research department there may be statisticians, interviewers, librarians, and data processing people. A company might have an entire group of people whose job it is to forecast sales. These are just a few of the many possible types of positions within the marketing field. Additional job titles may be found in chapter 7,

"Advancing Your Career," and in the discussion of entry-level qualifications that follows. For more information on marketing management positions, refer to an excellent book called *Job Descriptions in Marketing Management* by JoAnne Sperling (American Management Association Research Study 94, New York, 1964).

QUALIFICATIONS AND ENTERING THE FIELD

As with sales, there is no one set of qualifications for marketing positions. This is because there are so many different jobs in marketing, so many different ways to get into the field (through a position in sales or through an MBA, for example), and different companies in the same industry that are hiring for similar positions may have fairly divergent requirements.

Marketing is a highly conceptual field and so an ability to deal with abstract ideas is important. Writing ability is also helpful. This means more than just spelling and grammar; it means an ability to construct a complex argument. For these reasons, a college degree is a preferred qualification but not an absolute requirement. A knowledge of psychology, sociology, business, and quantitative techniques like statistical analysis and research skills are extremely valuable too. A college degree that combines several of these disciplines is excellent preparation for a career in marketing.

In addition to a college degree (good grades are a must), many companies also prefer or require an MBA—especially for positions in brand management and market research. An MBA is also extremely helpful for advancement to higher marketing positions. Two additional, frequently mentioned qualifications are experience in sales and experience in the particular industry. Almost all spokespeople in the field indicate that they look for "doers" who have imagination, who are good at what they do, and who can do a lot of different things.

There are a number of different ways to enter the field of marketing. One of the major ways is through a college or MBA program placement office. The placement office usually will have listings of companies looking for marketing trainees. In addition, many companies send on-campus recruiters to interview college grads or MBAs. Some companies have summer intern programs for college students. Check the major companies in your area.

Sales is a second major way to enter marketing management. In fact, many companies like to have marketing people work in sales before moving into other aspects of marketing.

Any experience with a product or customer may be a stepping-stone to marketing. Customer service is one area. For example, an individual can start working in equipment maintenance, become a field service supervisor, be promoted in customer service management and then, perhaps with additional education, move into other areas of marketing.

Any experience even in a support capacity in any of the function areas can lead to a position in marketing. Many secretarial, administrative assistant or receptionist positions have been the springboards into marketing positions. There is no set route.

When looking for marketing jobs, it's best to know the exact operational structure of the specific companies to which you would like to apply. When researching, check to see if the marketing department has its own personnel department; many do. It's best if you apply to or do your research directly with the marketing department itself rather than through a general personnel division.

To decide what area of marketing is best for you, study your background and analyze your strengths. If you have a strong statistical background, you might decide on market research—even if your first job will be as a tabulator. If you've worked for a company—even in a secretarial or administrative capacity—that distributed products or that is a wholesaler, then consider applying to the product distribution department of one of the companies whose products your employer has handled.

If you are determined and creative, you'll be successful.

Below is a list of sample entry-level marketing positions based on a survey of some of the basic industry areas. This list is meant to provide a rough idea of types of qualifications for marketing positions. Bear in mind that different companies within the same industry may have substantially different qualifications.

SOME ENTRY-LEVEL MARKETING POSITIONS AND THEIR REQUIREMENTS

Industry:
  Textiles
Position:
  Range from: merchandising, production control, production scheduling, sales records, personnel, planning, budgeting and forecasting.
Qualifications:
  —Prefer MBA but will hire with just college degree.
  —Grades are very important. Minimum acceptable

grade point average is 3.0 out of 4.0.

—Only position where MBA is required is in market research. Advertising or merchandising doesn't require an MBA.

—Prefer people with experience in textiles, manufacturing or marketing.

—Personality is important. Person must be adaptable. Must deal with people in a variety of levels in and outside of the company. For example, a person involved in market research goes to trade association meetings and must deal with other companies' chief executive officer, etc.

—There is no training program.

—Successful career path in marketing—one way to rise: start in sales, move to production control or planning or scheduling, become an assistant sales or merchandising manager, become vice president.

Industry:

Plastics

Position:

Product manager, marketing service manager, public relations, merchandising, advertising

Qualifications:

—College degree required. MBA helpful but not required. Grades decrease in importance with greater experience.

—Experience required, usually 2 years of selling experience or other marketing background.

—Seek individuals who are energetic and ambitious.

—Training is done by division.

—A successful person would have a background in research development, or manufacturing.

—The company seeks personnel with diverse backgrounds for marketing positions.

Industry:

Canned/Cured/Frozen Foods

Position:

Not specified

Qualifications:

—Prefer MBA *and* experience—such as experience with an ad agency, in the consumer product industry, or with a market research firm. Grades are considered but do not predominate. MBA without experience is not as desirable. Working for a competitor or in sales or financing is also good experience.

—Stress good verbal and written skills.

—No formal training program but the company tries to expose people to different brands by rotating them.

—A successful career path could be taken by one who starts as a product assistant, then associate product manager to product manager, to group product manager, to general manager's position.

Industry:

Drugs

Position:

Marketing associate, associate product manager, assistant product manager, product manager, group product manager.

Qualifications:

—Requires MBA and 2 years of experience—preferably in marketing; will accept sales experience.

—Marketing people go through sales training as part of their orientation, but there is no marketing training program.

—Marketing includes advertising, as well as coordinating with legal and regulatory personnel, and putting on symposiums.

Industry:

Grain Mill Products

Position:

Market associate, market assistant

Qualifications:

—For the market associate position they require no MBA. For the market assistant position an MBA is needed. Grades in college for both positions are very important.

—Experience is not required.

—Looking for dynamic personable type.

—Training program depends on level of education. Those with only a college degree must spend approximately 6 months in marketing, a few months in market research, and a few months in operations before they become an assistant brand manager.

—Those with an MBA require no training.

—Successful career path, for example: assistant brand manager, for approximately 1-1½ years, then product group manager, for approximately 2-3 years.

Industry:

Construction and Machinery

Positions:

Trainee field representative, supervisor, instructor

Qualifications:

—No MBA required at entry level. Prefer college degree with study in area of marketing or engineering. Grades important.

—No experience required.

—Looking for the person who is "ready to meet the

public" and who was active in school organizations.

—Same training as sales (18 weeks in classroom).

Industry:

Household Appliances

Position:

Advertising, market research, product evaluation, product order, service department

Qualifications:

—No MBA needed. College degree may be required depending on level of experience.

—Experience not required.

—Seeking people with good communications skills and with research and analytic skills.

—3 months training before starting job.

Industry:

Chemicals

Position:

Sales manager, product manager, assistant district manager, district manager, general manager for a division

Qualifications:

—Must have college degree; MBA not required.

—Experience with sales is a must. People in marketing must have experience in sales first.

—Interested in individual who expresses interest in career development in marketing.

—No training program.

Industry:

Furniture

Position:

Assistant sales manager

Qualifications:

—No MBA or college degree required, but most have college education.

—Experience not required.

—View how person comes across. Stress personal interview and are interested in an applicant's background.

—Prefer local people.

—6 months training to learn all phases of factory process. Informal office training.

Industry:

Industrial, Engineering, Scientific, Mechanical

Position:

Marketing specialist, products specialist

Qualifications:

—Education not as important as experience (most high-tech companies look for experience in electronic and computer industries).

—Prefer someone with a BS in marketing and also are receptive to people with MBA, but MBA not

required.

—Experience is essential. Looking for 3-5 years experience in marketing.

—Looking for assertive person who has insight and can deal with people well; need strong business sense and the ability to anticipate future needs.

Industry:

Computers

Position:

Product marketing manager

Qualifications:

—No entry-level positions. Require an MBA and a technical degree.

—Experience is essential. Experience in standard product marketing, product introduction and product life cycle management.

—No training program.

Industry:

Market Research/Special Market Analysis

Position:

Market researcher

Qualifications:

—Does not require an MBA.

—General college degree adequate.

—Prefer experience with market research department of another company or with an advertising agency.

—Want applicants to have prior knowledge of the field.

—No training program.

Industry:

Market Research/Audience Auditing

Position:

Market researcher

Qualifications:

—Take people directly out of college.

—Doesn't require an MBA

—Liberal Arts course of study is fine.

—No experience required; but prefer someone who has had an internship in the field.

—Looking for people who have analytic or quantitative backgrounds; excellent communication skills.

—Must be able to work in a "team environment."

—No training program: on-the-job training.

INDUSTRIAL TRAINING SERVICES

LAURA SUSKI is market sector manager with Xerox Learning Systems in Stamford, Connecticut, a part of Xerox Corporation that develops and sells training programs to other companies, including over 400 of the "Fortune 500." Laura, who has an MBA in marketing from Harvard Business School, joined XLS as a marketing planning analyst. She was promoted in turn to assistant product manager and product manager—and then to her present job where she is responsible for new product development and growth management of her market sector—the sales training area. Other market sectors at Xerox Learning Systems include management training, customer service training, and supervisory training. All the market sector managers report to the vice president of marketing.

Laura's primary product is called Professional Selling Skills and she is responsible for setting pricing strategy, for packaging and positioning the product, for advertising and for sales support.

"Industrial marketing—marketing to other companies—is different from consumer marketing," Laura says. "Because the needs of our clients are so complex, we are more dependent on our sales force to develop business, analyze our clients' needs and make recommendations for using our products: it is aimed at specific decision makers within companies of certain sizes and industries. Commercial or industrial marketing is now using many of the research and measurement techniques pioneered by consumer products companies."

"If you've got marketing or selling experience and demonstrated success in selling intangibles, then you would be considered for associate product manager," she says. "That's the entry-level position right now. Also, you might be eligible for a sales position."

Laura noted that in a fast-growing company like hers, jobs are created all the time—and they change very quickly. "It's a fluid situation," she said. "And that means there's a lot of opportunity for people coming in. Jobs are created as they are needed, presenting options for new career paths."

6
Job Finding Primer

DECIDING on a position or changing a job is an important career move—one of the most important you will ever have to make. Your job is more than just a source of income or the place where you spend as much as one third of your life. It is part of who you are and who you are becoming; it is—or should be—a source of satisfaction and self-esteem. For some people, job hunting is viewed simply as a matter of typing up a resume, answering ads, signing up with an employment agency, waiting for offers, and then choosing from among offers. While this approach can be successful, it may cause you to neglect an opportunity to decide what you really want to do and what you most have to offer. Job hunting is an opportunity to go out and find the job you really want, rather than hoping that it will find you! It can be an exciting and rewarding challenge—if you are willing to put imagination and active effort into it.

In this chapter you'll learn how to determine what kind of job you want, and then how to go about finding it. To assist you in performing some of the career exercises that are part of this chapter, we suggest that you also read the next chapter, "Advancing Your Career," with specific attention to the section on developing a career advancement plan and to using the Career Advancement Journal. The planning and journal technique should be used to keep an ongoing record of your job hunting process.

CLARIFYING YOUR OBJECTIVES

If you do not know where you want to go, how will you get there or know when you have arrived? Clarifying your career destination is the first and most important step on your job campaign. Job objectives are what you want out of your job, no matter what position you have.

Try to be as realistic as you can about your objectives. Many people are likely to say that they want a creative, responsible job with plenty of independent work, and perhaps some supervising responsibilities. But such objectives may not suit your particular personality; they may, for example, be too demanding. While you do not want to overreach yourself when setting objectives, at the same time you will not want to settle for too little, either. If you must err, err on the side of setting your sights a little too high, rather than too low.

Get a pencil and several sheets of paper and find a quiet place to work, away from distractions. Ask yourself "What do I really want out of my job, no matter what kind of job I have?" To answer this question, write down anything that comes to mind, no matter how trivial or grandiose. Do not be shy about wanting to earn $100,000 a year or wanting a job in which you work alone. Draw up a list of your short-term and long-term objectives.

In setting your personal objectives, you will have to balance your personal desires with your practical needs, such as your budget. And, in identifying the things that are truly important to you, try to be as specific as possible without narrowing your possibilities too much. Throw away your preconceptions and do not let them make up your mind for you.

There are scores of objectives career planners might have. Here are a few topic ideas to get you started. Topic headings can often help you to generate more specific objectives.

Salary	Duties
Benefits	Job Title/Prestige
Responsibility Level	Pressure Level
Supervisory Level	Hours/Overtime
Growth Potential	Writing
Office Environment	Intellectual Demands
Co-workers	Creativity
Location	Pace
Detail Level	Diversity
People Contact	Complexity
Subject Matter/Industry	

Compensation. What is the minimum salary/compensation you need to conform to your current or projected budget? How much more do you want to make? How much are you willing to sacrifice to earn this level? Why? What else do you want/need to spend the money on? Once you have asked yourself these questions, then specify a salary range for yourself.

Responsibility. Responsibility is a two-edged sword. It can be a challenge and a burden at the same time. Are you willing to accept the burden that goes with the challenge?

Office Environment. Is office environment important to you? Do you need a plush office, with artwork on the walls and a view of the city? Do you want to work at a small firm where you will know all your colleagues, or would you prefer a large corporation with greater diversity? Do you prefer a casual atmosphere where people are on a first-name basis, or a formal office where a three-piece suit is *de rigueur*?

Supervision. Do you like to work independently and to solve your own problems? Or do you feel more comfortable with assigned or supervised tasks?

Location. Do you mind commuting to work? Would

you sacrifice other objectives if you could walk to the office?

Hours. What is the best work schedule for you? Do you have a strong preference for flexible hours? Evaluate the amount of extra work you'll have to put in each day to accomplish your career objectives. Is the extra time really worth it to you?

Typical Duties. What do you like to do at work? Most people live for the highlights of their jobs, but they have to live with the day-to-day too. What kinds of things would you most like to do, what would you not mind doing and what would you not like to do? If you are currently employed, ask these questions about your own job.

Job Title and Prestige. If your job title and the prestige that goes along with it are important to you, write this down. If you have gone to medical school in part for the "M.D." after your name, it is a legitimate objective for you.

Your Life After Work. If home, family, hobbies, entertainment and relaxing are very important parts of your life, then you will probably not want a job that will make too many demands beyond set working hours. If you must be challenged in your work, then be prepared to adjust your priorities around your job.

Dozens of other job objectives might occur to you. The important thing is to establish them so that you can work with them. For each objective, ask yourself the kinds of questions we have just asked, and test them to see how firm and important they are.

If you are having trouble clarifying your job objectives, and if you are dissatisfied with your present situation, use that knowledge as a starting point. If you are working now, and if you feel your salary is too low, pinpoint an ideal but realistic salary. If your work is too routine, ask yourself what tasks you would find exciting and challenging. Let your imagination work.

Finally, rank the objectives that you have listed, in order of importance to you. No one can answer this for you, so trust your own instincts, and be honest. If salary is your most important objective, say so. If you would be willing to sacrifice a higher salary for more prestige, indicate this. You may find that as you work through this process, your objectives will change. Great! You are in the process of discovering what you really want.

Throughout your job search, refer back to your list. You should constantly ask yourself, as you research potential employers and jobs, how your objectives are being met.

TAKING STOCK OF YOURSELF—WHAT YOU HAVE TO OFFER

Taking stock of yourself is another important part of the job hunting process. And it can be a very satisfying one, as when you discover that you have more to offer than you ever imagined. The key to doing this well is not to overlook any positive qualities that you have. In this process of taking stock of yourself, you can develop an insight into who you are, and this will be useful to you in writing your resume, in interviewing and in your daily professional life.

Suppose you have raised a family and have not worked for years; you still have much to offer. Managing a home and family can be more difficult than running a small business. You have to budget time and money, assume a great deal of responsibility and solve problems. And that is only part of it. Add in your work for the PTA, local charity, or religious or political organization. Perhaps you have traveled abroad, helped to sell your house, or are particularly patient and understanding. No matter who you are or what you have done, you are likely to have so much to offer that it may be difficult to know where to begin.

Taking stock of yourself is another pencil and paper exercise. Once again you will need a quiet place, free from distractions, to consider what you have to offer.

Write down everything that comes to mind. And for each quality that you note, provide an illustrative example or two. Do not focus too much on your present job or the lack of one. Also do not gear your thinking only to a specific employer or job category.

You might begin by dividing your skills inventory into four broad areas: personal skills, professional, education, and memberships and credentials.

Personal Skills

The most important thing you bring to a career campaign is *yourself*—not your resume or your job title, but who you are as a person. A personal skill is anything you have to offer—school, business, friendships, family, hobbies, sports—that helps you to succeed. There is a lot of overlap between personal and career skills, but the accent here is on personality. Do not worry whether a personal skill seems applicable to a job. The important point is this: everyone has personal skills; it is just a question of clarifying them. All those traits that have made you a successful father, mother, friend, athlete, hobbyist or student can make you an equally successful—for the purposes of this book—sales representative, sales manager, or market researcher.

Of course, there are plenty of personal skills; here is just a partial list to get you started:

reliability	taking criticism well	empathy
honesty	self-confidence	speaking voice
loyalty	desire to succeed	vocabulary
concentration	handling pressure	appearance
congeniality	patience	decisiveness
organizational	travel	ability to listen
ability	handling responsibility	good with details
quick learning		

How many more can you think of?

Professional Skills

Professional skills are those skills more closely associated with demonstrable abilities you have used on the job, or which might be included as a job requirement. Of course, many jobs also require personal skills, such as organization ability or people ability. Do not worry if there is some duplication. And do not skip over this section, even if you think you already know the answers. Write down *every* task, area of knowledge and major achievement connected with your current job and every other job you have had. Next to each skill write down a "proof" or two.

If you are in sales now, this list might include the types of products you have sold, the sales methods you have used (like cold calling or group-presentation) and your technical knowledge. In marketing it might include the market research analysis techniques you know, the types of packaging you've worked with, planning techniques you're familiar with for new product introduction, product distribution planning, etc.

You should even list skills developed through hobbies. Have you tinkered with electronics or developed your own photographs? Such hobby knowledge might help you land a job. The skills you have developed in one area can often be transferred to another.

Education

There are hundreds of things you have learned about in school, at seminars, or from other special classes. Any of these could be of interest to an employer. For example, your French, which you practiced on your summer vacation; or your math skills, which helped with some kind of business computations. Some of your skills may be just waiting for the right opportunity for use. Perhaps those biology classes you took once may help qualify you for a job in sales or marketing of medical products, or that evening seminar on investing in the stock market may help qualify you for a job in a financial services company.

The best place to begin is with your high school, college and graduate school transcripts. Consider every course. Note them on your list. Now look at all the special seminars and continuing education classes that you have taken. Try to list the skills you have learned and the abilities you have developed. Through an English course you might have learned how to write well or how to do library research and use source materials. If you have done well in certain areas, be sure to include this as proof of your talent and ability.

Memberships and Credentials

Memberships and credentials may be another area in which you will discover skills and experience. These demonstrate your interests and accomplishments. Your participation in a charity organization, for example, might easily indicate skills that are transferable to another type of organization. Naturally, you should list professional organizations like the Sales Executive Club or the Association of MBAs. List all your memberships and then consider what you contributed and learned, and what you have to offer.

Review

To put your compiled lists into perspective, go back through them all and rate your relative strengths in each area. How much does each skill or area of knowledge appeal to you? Do you like what you are good at—and vice versa? Think back over your objectives, too. How do your skills and experience coincide with these?

One last step. Once you have taken stock in yourself, you must be able to sell yourself to yourself before you can sell yourself to someone else. In the process thus far, you may have left off your lists things that you do not like or that you are not particularly good at. If there are areas in which you have had an opportunity to see that you are not very good, if there are things you really do not like, put these down on a separate list. If the job you seek requires you to utilize skills and abilities you do not like or have, then you may have to reconsider your priorities. At the same time, be sure you don't overlook all your positive skills, abilities and talents.

IDENTIFYING JOB POSSIBILITIES

Identifying job possibilities is where your objectives —what you want—and your skills—what you have to offer—come together. Finding a job that fits your needs, and needs your skills, is the acid test of a realistic career pursuit. Before you start interviewing for positions or answering ads, draw up a list of possible jobs you would like to explore. Investigate these jobs as specifically as possible to find out what they offer, what they involve and what they require. Of course, some information can only be acquired from an interview. But you may find out a lot by talking with people already in such positions or by doing some library research.

You might find yourself with a dearth of job ideas; if so, you may have to spend more time reviewing your list of objectives and skills. They can be useful in narrowing your choices, but they can also be used to generate job ideas. If you cannot come up with job ideas, be creative. Do not be embarrassed to list ideas you think of as silly or farfetched. If your ultimate dream is to be a film star, you might now consider a sales or marketing position in the film industry.

If you want more ideas, check the other sections in the book. Refer to the "Using Directories, Periodicals and Reference Books" section that appears later in this chapter. An hour in the library might prompt some new ideas. The important thing is to be honest with yourself—honest about your objectives and honest about your skills.

YOUR RESUME—THE 45-SECOND COMMERCIAL

Your resume is an advertisement—for you. Think of your job search as a marketing campaign. All the skills and experience you had when taking stock of yourself are what your prospective employer buys when you are hired.

A resume is one of your most effective sales tools. Its purpose is not, however, to get you a job. The resume is designed to get you an interview, and it is on the basis of how well you interview that you will get an offer. Of course, your resume may form the basis for discussion during your interview and you can, by referring to your resume, control the questions asked.

A resume is a 45-second commercial because 45 seconds is about how long it takes for the eye to skim an average resume. During those 45 seconds, a decision is being made, consciously or unconsciously, by the reader. Either your resume captures the reader's interest, makes him want to consider it in closer detail, or your reader's attention fades and he files the resume away with all the others. The person reading your resume probably reads many others and does not study each one in depth; his job is to select the few from the many. Will he or she select yours? You stand an excellent chance of having yours selected if you have written a good one.

As an ad, your resume is geared to a specific market, to the type of job you want or to the field in which you are seeking employment. What you put into your resume is what your prospective market should want to see. A resume is not a biography that tells your life story or what is most important *to you* about yourself.

If the types of jobs you are looking for are very different from each other, you may need more than one resume—especially if the skills and experience valued by each are different. For example, let us say you are a medical sales representative now and plan on seeking another sales position or a sales management position. Most likely, you'll need two resumes.

Appearance, Paper and Length

Before an employer even reads your resume, he sees and touches it. A resume is more than a collection of words. It is also a visual, tactile product that makes a statement about you, just as much as your own appearance.

Paper. Use a high quality bond paper, perhaps 25% rag. It might cost a little more, but it will indicate your professionalism. Choose gray, white or cream. Orange or fuchsia or other bright colors are too loud. Match your envelopes with the same paper stock used for your resume and cover letters.

Layout. Your resume should be designed so that it is restful on the eye and easy to read. A clean typeface, spacious organization, good use of headlines and underscoring will help your resume make sense. As your resume is scanned, the reader should be able to pick out items of interest quickly. Therefore, each section should be visually separate, and each point easy to find. Also, do not cram too much onto the page.

Have your resume typed on a high-quality machine, such as an IBM Selectric. It should go without saying that there must be *no* grammatical, spelling or typographic mistakes, smudges or obvious typed corrections. Your resume should look as presentable as *you* will! After all, if you do not care enough to do the best job possible on your resume, should an employer trust you with his work?

If you have put all the work you should into your resume, you will want it to look really good. Since you will need more than one copy, perhaps 25-50 or more, you will need a way to reproduce the resume. The best quality, lowest cost method is photo-offset. To prepare a resume for photo-offset, you can type it on plain white paper. Call an offset house to find out the details. Or, today there are a few photocopy machines that are capable of high-quality printing—provided they are kept in top working order. You might be able to have your resume reproduced this way, on the kind of paper you have chosen.

Length. Your resume is best if it is only on one page—unless you have a lot of experience or an unusual situation. If you need more space, use a second page, but no more. Leave something left to say at the interview.

The Resume-Writing Process

The first step in writing the resume is to gather your list of personal and professional skills as we discussed in the "Taking Stock of Yourself" section. Look the list over carefully and check whether there is anything you wish to add. If you are in doubt about whether something is valuable, list it for now anyway.

The next step is to rework this list. Using each skill

as a topic heading, list a few of the important ways each of your skills can be substantiated. Then go through your jobs and experience. For each, list your regular duties and any special projects. Also list any special accomplishments or highlights. You will always find something that stands out. Do the same for your education.

The third step is to identify the skills and requirements of the jobs for which you wish to apply and to match your personal skills accordingly. Leave off the skills, accomplishments and details that you now see are unimportant.

Now you are ready to organize and edit your skills and experience into a one-page resume, or at most, two-page resume. Use either the chronological resume or the functional resume format. (Samples of each follow on pages 64-81.)

Style. The prose style of your resume should be vital, active, and concise. Omit extra words. If you can cut out a word and still make sense of the resume, keep trimming until you can no longer understand it; then you will know that you have gone too far. You needn't use full sentences. The resume's prose style is less than telling a story and more than making a list. Use the simple past tense for everything but your objective, unless you are discussing an ongoing job or activity. For example: "Duties: cold calling prospect accounts and trained new sales staff." Don't write "My duties included cold calling on prospective accounts as well as training new sales personnel."

However, when pruning, do not cut out the little words that help cast you in a positive light. Every word or detail on your resume should help to sell you. Your resume is actually a story of your success and your skills: you "built," "revamped," "reorganized," "expanded," "improved," and so on.

The Chronological Resume

There are two basic types of resumes: the chronological resume and the functional resume. The resume which suits you best depends upon your work history, personal background, and the job you wish to find.

The chronological resume is the most commonly used format. It is called chronological because it lists your professional experiences in *reverse chronological order*: your most *recent* job first, your previous job next, etc. The chronological resume is the easiest to write. If your job history is straightforward and fairly well in line with your job objective, by all means use the reverse chronological resume. If you are uncertain about whether the chronological or functional resume is better, stay with the former. The same holds true if you are not sure you can write a functional resume, often a tricky thing to do.

A reverse chronological resume has eight or nine sections: Contact, an optional Objective or Synopsis, Awards, Professional Skills, Education, Professional Experience, Memberships and Credentials, Interests, and References. Much of this information will also appear on the functional resume, so if you are interested in this second format, keep reading.

CONTACT

Contact information includes your name, written in neat, large letters; your address with zip code; and your telephone number with area code. Your name, address and phone number go at the top of the page. You can center all this information, or you might put your name on the left-hand side, and address and phone number on the right. You can print your name in boldface or caps, or underscore it. These are options you can choose; use whatever looks best. But do not leave your phone number off by mistake or misspell your own name!

OBJECTIVE OR SYNOPSIS

You may want to include an objective or synopsis; it is optional. You needn't use an objective if your skills and experience speak for themselves, but even then it can be useful. The job objective is one of the ways you can target yourself to a specific position. A typical objective might read "OBJECTIVE: Lightly experienced salesman seeks entry-level position." If you are an experienced sales professional trying to switch fields, then an objective might be very helpful. For example: "OBJECTIVE: Achievement-oriented sales professional with in-depth knowledge of breakfast cereals seeks responsible position in product management." An objective is also useful if you are seeking a management position.

A synopsis is a microcosm of your resume, highlighting your skills and experience. It tells the reader how he ought to perceive you. Later on in the resume you will prove it. Of course, you select what you want the potential employer to see. A synopsis is especially useful when you are making a big switch, when your skills and experience do not necessarily speak for themselves. It can also be used to underscore your skills, even if you don't think they need added emphasis. Often a synopsis and an objective can be combined in one entry. For example: "Dynamic sales professional experienced in microcomputer systems, training, and applications-design seeks growth position in management consulting." If you choose an objective or synopsis, keep it short. One line is best, three lines the maximum.

AWARDS

If you have won sales awards or industry recognition in marketing, say, list those in a separate section. For example:

SALES AWARDS

1979   Most New Accounts Opened
1981   Million Dollar Club
1982   Northeast Region Sales Leader

The awards section may come before or in place of the professional skills section depending upon the story you wish to tell. Unless you have several impressive awards, it may be best to place the awards section towards the end of your resume or to incorporate an award within the entry concerning the specific job in which you won the award.

PROFESSIONAL SKILLS

Since sales and marketing often involve knowledge of technical fields, your special skills are very important and are often the first item a prospective employer may look for on your resume. If you have an extensive roster of skills, then you might lead off with a laundry list of them. Such skills may include technical areas of knowledge, product lines, or sales techniques. For example, a marketing manager might list the following professional skills:

PROFESSIONAL SKILLS

Direct Mail Marketing   Conjoint Analysis Market
Telephone Marketing   Research
Product Distribution Planning   Sales Training

A sales representative might list the types of product lines or sales techniques with which he is familiar:

IBM Mainframes   Word Processing Systems
DEC Micro-Minis
High Speed Telephone
   Switching Equipment

If you do not yet have an impressive roster of skills, omit this section.

EDUCATION

Depending upon a number of factors, the next section highlights either your education or your professional experience. If you are currently employed, remaining in the same field, and have a straightforward, uncomplicated employment history, you'll usually list your work history first. Some job applicants, however, should put their education first: if you are a recent graduate applying for a first job; if you have graduated from an outstanding university, have an MBA, or have an exceptional academic background.

In general, if you consider your education more relevant than your experience, put your education first. A career changer who recently went back to school and completed a course in sales, marketing or a technical field might want to list education before employment.

The education section should include schools you have attended, degrees earned, academic honors won, important extracurricluar activities, and your dates of attendance or graduation. The dates can either appear in the left-hand margin before the name of the school or after the school and degree listing. Always list your highest degree, or most recent educational experience, first. A college graduate does not need to include the name of his high school. If you have not attended college, or did not graduate, include your high school and any post-graduate or vocational training. College graduates sometimes enter their grade-point averages. This is recommended only if your grades are outstanding.

PROFESSIONAL EXPERIENCE

The work-history section of a chronological resume should list all your jobs, including volunteer positions, in reverse chronological order. The section is usually signaled by a headline, often in uppercase letters and underlined, reading: "EXPERIENCE," "PROFESSIONAL EXPERIENCE," or "WORK EXPERIENCE." You can list the name and address of the company first on one line, followed by your job title on the next. You can underline your job title and/or company name, or place them in capital letters. It is unnecessary to include the firm's complete mailing address; the name of the city and state are sufficient. The dates of your employment are best placed in the left-hand margin. Do not bother to include the days you worked; the month and year are enough.

If you worked for a well-known corporation, there is no need to elaborate upon the nature of its business. For lesser-known companies, it can be useful to indicate something about the size and scope of the business, e.g., "retail firm with $3.8 million annual sales"; "manufacturer of abrasives and solvents"; "fourth largest commercial real estate broker in Orlando."

Every job listing should be followed by a concise, pertinent description of your duties and, then, major accomplishments. If you have an extensive enough roster of duties and special achievements, you may use these as subheads and list the duties under one paragraph and the accomplishments under another. Space is at a premium in your resume. Try not to let a job entry exceed ten to fifteen lines. Keep the descriptions relevant, and phrase them to emphasize your accomplishments. It's best if each new item, duty, accomplishment, or responsibility begins on a new line. If the item needs more than one line, you might consider indenting its continuation on the next line. This will help keep the presentation clear.

MEMBERSHIPS AND CREDENTIALS

The section on memberships and credentials can be important. It can indicate that you are a "doer," especially if you have been an officer, a coordinator or a committee functionary.

Credentials include any licenses or certifications that you might have. As with memberships, they indicate your accomplishments and the scope of your activities.

INTERESTS

Special skills and interests should be included in your resume if they indicate unusual accomplishments or the mastery of a subject or a skill that is potentially applicable to a business. No employer cares that you like to ski, travel, or listen to records. He would perhaps be impressed, however, if you were an accomplished skier or an electrical hobbyist. These indicate that you have mastered an interest, a sign of your dedication and intelligence. Some skills or interest, such as language ability, could be of value to a firm or business. Others, like athletic accomplishments, could be helpful in indicating your expertise in a difficult skill. If you list interests, do not refer to them as "hobbies"; the word connotes superficial entertainment, rather than serious pursuits.

REFERENCES

The final part of the resume is your reference section. Despite the name of this section, *you don't list your references*. The customary procedure is to use the phrase, "References available upon request," or something similar. Of course, you should make certain that your references are willing to recommend you before you provide their names to a prospective employer.

The Functional Resume

The functional resume can be a helpful tool for some job finders. It repackages and presents what you have to offer in terms of your talents, rather than chronological dates. It is especially useful if your skills and experience do not fit into a cumulative or straightforward pattern. The functional resume is a preferable style for a number of situations. If you are returning to the job market after a long hiatus from paid employment, you will want to stress your abilities and general experience rather than your work history. If you are changing career fields, a functional resume would also be a good idea. Instead of emphasizing that you have worked seven years in an unrelated field, say, you can stress the skills and experience that are relevant to the job you seek. The functional resume allows you to do this.

Functional and chronological resumes are basically formatted the same way in all areas except for professional experience. Here, instead of a section made up of subsections that focus on each of the several jobs you may have had, each subsection focuses on a specific skill or particular type of job. You might even call this section professional skills. For each heading or entry, you will have gathered *all* the relevant experience you have had.

For example, let us say that you are applying for a word processing (WP) sales position and that you have been a WP secretary in a law firm. While in school, you once had a part-time job selling clothes in a retail store, on commission. After an objective, your first entry in the professional skills section might be "Sales." Under this head you should discuss your success in selling and your knowledge of sales techniques, as well as any special on-the-job training you had. If you were one of the best salespeople in the store, mention it. You might also include any experience you have had in "selling" new programs or procedures to your previous managers. If you are or have been a speaker or leader in a membership organization, mention it, for such work also involves sales skills.

Your next entry in the professional skills section might read "Knowledge of WP." As an experienced operator, you probably know a lot. Finally, you may want to include a special "Law Firm" section, since this area might be the market to whom you will sell the WP equipment. As a legal secretary, you may also have been involved in purchasing equipment and may already understand this process. If so, indicate this.

In the above example, we have tried to indicate how you draw all your skills and experience together to work best for you. From the WP profile, the secretary now seems like a natural for a sales position. You should use the functional resume to make yourself seem a natural, too.

After you have completed the professional skills section, you then have to indicate that your skills have been acquired through employment. Therefore, follow this section with a brief section on employment history or work experience. This will list, in reverse chronological order, your previous employer, even if you were a volunteer, and your job titles. Dates of employment are optional, but they should probably be included, unless you have had significant employment gaps. You may also want to rephrase a previous job title to fit in with your current job goals.

Tips for Resume Writers

We have included below some sample resumes to help you with your own. Use them as guidelines only. Your resume should be a little different from everyone else's to reflect what is unique and special about you. In preparing your resume, consider this list of "Do's and Do nots":

- Do not refer to yourself by name or with "I" in the job description section of your resume.
- Do not include unnecessary and unsolicited personal information about yourself, such as your health, marital status, religion, politics, number of children, or date of birth.
- Do not send out a resume with spelling or grammatical errors.
- Do not send out a resume that is smudged or poorly reproduced.
- Do not include a photo of yourself, or decorative graphics on your resume.
- Do not give reasons for leaving previous jobs.
- Do not list a salary or earning objective,. or your previous earnings.
- Do not list the names of supervisors.
- Do leave plenty of margins.
- Do use a resume writer's poetic license to present yourself in a favorable light, but do not stretch the truth until it breaks.

**A sample of a chronological resume, excellent for someone
who wishes to advance within the same field.**

Jean Ellen Deter

118 East Madison Avenue
Collingswood, New Jersey 08108
(609) 858-6636

EXPERIENCE

5/79 -   CRM/DUNLEE, INC., Elizabeth, New Jersey
Present

5/81 -   Marketing Analyst
Present   Responsibilities:
            --prepare and evaluate analysis of monthly, quarterly and annual
              sales and marketing data
            --calculate sales budgets, product lines and territories, and
              incentive compensation for six sales forces
            Achievements:
            --implemented conversion of management reports from manual to
              computer execution
            --produced in-depth study of major competitors and made promotional
              and pricing recommendations based upon study
            --contributed to reorientation of marketing strategies after
              divisional reorganization

9/80 -   Supervisor, Promotional Department
5/81   Responsibilities:
            --coordinate all aspects of direct mail and space advertising
              production; trade show and film festival participation
            --research new mailing lists for direct mail campaigns
            --supervise maintenance of mailing lists from direct mail responses
            Achievements:
            --reorganized method of promotion response analysis to enable
              more accurate interpretation of data
            --instituted more efficient procedures for maintaining correct
              inventory level of film study guides for over 600 films

5/79 -   Assistant to Senior Product Manager
9/80   --assist in production of direct mail campaigns

EDUCATION

University of Michigan, Ann Arbor, Michigan
  B.A. in Linguistics, cum laude, (1978)

Special Training: University of California, San Diego
  EDP Courses in BASIC, COBOL

PROFESSIONAL
MEMBERSHIPS

Direct Mail Marketing Club of Southern California

References available upon request.

A sample of a functional resume. This resume shows how someone with light sales experience but in-depth knowledge of word processing can repackage his or her skills to qualify for an entry sales position in word processing.

ALICE PETERSON

Old Indian Village Road   715-588-3686
Lee Du Flambeau, Wisconsin 07409

OBJECTIVE: Dynamic WP professional with sales savvy seeks entry position in word processing sales.

PROFESSIONAL SKILLS

Sales
Won "Number 1 Sales Rep" award for greatest sales volume.

Mastered basic sales techniques including: probing, handling objections, closing, cold call canvassing, product demonstration, and use of A/V sales aides.

Increased sales by more than 15% two years running.

Word Processing
Coordinated purchase and installation of 15 station WP/OIS for major bank. Developed systems specification for RFP. Contacted vendors, evaluated proposals and made final purchase recommendation.

Developed internal WP systems and applications for work flow management and handling specific bank functions (includes boilerplate, forms, and operating manuals).

Developed WP training programs for teaching basic WP skills and specific WP department procedures.

EMPLOYMENT HISTORY

1979-   First Bank of Wisconsin, Rhinelander, Wisconsin
Present   Executive Secretary; Secretarial Pool Supervisor; WP Supervisor

1977-   Smith's Department Store, Lee Du Flambeau, Wisconsin
1979   Cosmetic counter Commissioned Sales Representative

Summer,   Encyclopedia Britannica, Rhinelander, Wisconsin
1975   Door-to-door Sales Rep.

EDUCATION

1975-   Oneida Community College, Rhindelander, Wisconsin
1976   A.A. Business Communications
             Dean's List

MEMBERSHIPS: IWP, Chapter founder and Vice-President

References Available Upon Request.

Jeffrey Lewis
155 Main Line Drive
Toledo, Ohio 10399   Home: (213) 678-1822
                                        Business: (615) 382-3833

OBJECTIVE: Technical sales/research associate of pharmaceuticals or related
                 scientific products.

EDUCATION: Ohio State University. Columbus, Ohio.
                 M.S. Biological Life Sciences, 1980.
                 Member of Phi Alpha Zi. Honorary academic fraternity.
                 B.S. Agriculture/Business, 1977.
                 Financed expenses through part-time and summer work.

BUSINESS   MARKETING - Responsible for sales and market management of
EXPERIENCE: specialty group, proprietary pesticides in Northeastern, North
                 Central and Midwestern States. Representative for marketing
                 contract negotiations, investigations into claims and promotional
                 activities.

                 .Gave sales presentations. Prepared and conducted technical
                 sales meetings for distributors, dealers, consumer and trade
                 shows. Provided technical service, solved claims and other
                 problems associated with market introduction of new product.

                 .During first sales year of agricultural fungicide Funginex ^{R},
                 established sales of approximately $500,000.

                 RESEARCH AND DEVELOPMENT - Organized and coordinated field
                 research for experimental plant protection chemicals, and
                 continued development for registered products. Emphasis on
                 developing consumer use and precautionary instructions.

                 .Market research and research results, reporting to top
                 management.

                 .Experienced in SAS programming, biostatistics, experimental
                 design, laboratory and data analysis.

                 .Methodized and supervised further research and testing for
                 agricultural fungicide Funginex ^{R} for additional federal (EPA)
                 registrations and for plant growth regulator Curbiset ^{R} under
                 federal Experimental Use Permit protocol.

EMPLOYMENT:

1981-present   MARKETING/DEVELOPMENT SPECIALIST - MARTEX INDUSTRIES, INC., PLANT
                 PROTECTION DIVISION, HAWTHORNE, OHIO. Representatives of
                 DURKIN COMPANY, FRANKFURT, GERMANY. German manufacturer of plant
                 protection chemicals, annual worldwide sales of $150,000,000.

JOHN JONES
26 Watch Hill Avenue
Dallas, Texas 20110
(219) 338-2690

CAREER OBJECTIVE   To obtain a sales or marketing management position in a
progressive environment.

EXPERIENCE

3/78 - Present   Marketing Manager Equipment Division,
Simonex Corp., Garden City, New York

Managed marketing effort for all office equipment items manufactured. Wrote and executed annual marketing plan through
implementation of various product introductions, sales promotions and training seminars. Found new markets for existing
products as well as established and maintained a selective
distribution network for a staff support furniture system.
Provided direction to and monitored the efforts of advertising,
sales, production and engineering to ensure that the marketing
objectives put forth are reached.

3/77 - 3/78   Assistant Marketing Manager Equipment Division,
Simonex Corp., Garden City, New York

Developed statistical programs for evaluating new products and
market opportunities. Researched the market and competition,
test marketed products and trained sales force for national
distribution.

9/73 - 3/77   Sales Representative,
Melville Co., New York, New York

Responsible for the sale of pneumatic air tools in the New York
City, Long Island area. Played a key role in Melville's transition from a direct to end user marketing philosophy to a network
of industrial distributors.

2/72 - 9/73   Sales Correspondent,
Southern Screw & Bolt Corp., Dallas, Texas

Engaged in all activities necessary to answer technical
questions for customers and for providing field sales support.

EDUCATION

1976 - 1979   Graduate School of Business, University of Texas at Houston,
M.B.A. in Management.

1972 - 1976   New York Institute of Technology,
B.S. in Business Administration, Marketing major.

INTERESTS   Basketball, Racquetball, Long Distance Running

Thomas H. Watson
308 East 64th Street   Residence: (212) 863-4321
New York, N.Y. 10247   Business: (212) 245-4601

EXPERIENCE   Senior Customer Service Representative, Foreign Claims
INTOURIST CO.   Unit Travelers Check Division
May 1981 to Present   My responsibilities include interviewing customers who
                            have lost Travelers Checks; analyzing information pro-
                            vided to verify personal data from local law enforcement
                            agencies, government agencies and Intourist special
                            agents arranging refunds; reviewing Contract Violation
                            Claims; determining Forgeries and very heavy clerical
                            duties. In this unit I have also dealt heavily with
                            Foreign exchange rates and six different currency
                            Travelers Checks.

June 1980 -   Senior Customer Service Representative, Major Claims
May 1981   Travelers Check Division
                            My responsibilities in this unit covered Travelers
                            Check losses over $1,000 with a very high percentage
                            of Fraudulent Claims. It is in this unit I acquired
                            my interview technique. There was heavy verification
                            and investigations to determine the validity of claims.
                            Reviewing claims after paid checks had arrived and pre-
                            paring summaries for Management to make a decision.

August 1979 -   Correspondent, Redemption Unit, Travelers Check
May 1980   Division
                            Customer Service Representative dealing with Travelers
                            Checks belonging to customers who had either died or
                            become incompetent; large volume of telephone inquiries,
                            legal documents of Probate and Court appointments; and
                            heavy contact with Banks.

MARTIN'S DEPARTMENT STORES Assistant Manager
June 1978 - June 1979   Men's Apparel.

BARNETTE BROTHERS CO.
April 1978 - June 1978   Assistant to Merchandise Manager of Juvenile Wear

AMERICAN SCHOLARSHIP FUND
August 1977 - March 1978   Assistant to Director

ENVIRONMENTAL FUND PELHAM
MEMORIAL CAMP   Counselor & Art Teacher
June 1975 - August 1977

EDUCATION

Present   Pace University of N.Y. Matriculated for B.A.,
                            General Business. Intourist Education Program.

January 1975 -   Morrisville College, Morrisville, New York
December 1976   Degree: Associates Liberal Arts
                            Major: Liberal Arts
                            Minor: Business & Communications

Boris Pasternak
126 Arrowhead Lane
Oakland, N.J. 07436
(201) 733-4621

OBJECTIVE   Management Trainee or Accounting entry position with a
                     progressive company.

EDUCATION   Bachelor of Science, Fordham University, Bronx, N.Y.,
                     May 1983. Accounting major.

                     Don Bosco Preparatory High School, Ramsey, N.J.
                     Graduated 53rd in a class of 188

EMPLOYMENT

September 1982   Bethesda University. Coordinated circulation of the
to Present   University newspaper (The Phoenix) to various campuses.
                     Presented Editor with a study showing salaries could be
                     increased to cover actual expenses and yet remain within
                     budget. Developed more efficient delivery routes. Also
                     serve as Staff Photographer for the school paper and the
                     yearbook.

Summer 1982   IBM. Security Guard in the Mooristown, N.J. complex.
                     Performed internal audits and coordinated security
                     operations from command post.

Summer 1981   Quickstop Markets. Cashier/Night Manager, Midland Park,
                     N.J. Duties included cash reconciliations and inventory
                     audits.

Spring 1981   Tax Assistance Board of Greater New York. Assisted in
                     preparing income tax reports for a South Bronx Community
                     program.

Summer 1980   Stevenson's Inc. Mechanics Assistant at the Garfield,
                     N.J. Research Laboratories.

PERSONAL DATA   Fordham University Accounting Society.
                     Tennis, Track, and Weight Lifting.
                     Avid interest in Zoology.

References furnished upon request.

Pat M. Burns
2 Elmwood Avenue
Larchmont, N.Y. 10463
(914) 833-2781

EMPLOYMENT

1980-Present   Manager of Administrative Services
                Benson's Dry Goods Corp.
                New York, N.Y. 10016

                Reversed trend of increasing telecommunications costs.
                Coordinated 25,000 sq. ft. office renovation.
                Responsible for corporate office security and safety.

                Supervise general office operations, including:
                Telecommunications, Facilities Planning, Budgeting, Purchasing,
                Implementation of Word Processing, In-Plant Printing Facility,
                Security, Safety, Mailroom, Supply Room, Sample Room and
                Maintenance.

1970 - 1980   Purchasing/Services Manager
                International Center for Modern Art
                New York, N.Y. 10021

                Eliminated departmental deficit within six months.
                Reorganized warehouse operation and eliminated deficit.
                Directed relocation of staffs of two office buildings.

                Responsibilities included Administrative Services, Purchasing,
                Mail-Order Warehouse Operation, Reception, Managing Offset
                Department and Telecommunications. Technical Consultation to
                the Security Department.

1961 - 1970   Senior Buyer
                PCP Incorporated
                Middle Neck, N.Y. 11052

                Primary responsibilities were purchasing of military and
                commercial electronic components, office supplies and printing
                and general plant maintenance.

                EDUCATIONAL BACKGROUND

                B.A. Industrial Psychology, 1961
                Bard College
                Annandale-on-Hudson, N.Y.

                Specialized courses and seminars in business, including:
                    Purchasing Procedures
                    Business Law
                    Telecommunications
                    Word Processing
                    Purchase of Printing
                    Security Management (N.Y.P.D.)

                REFERENCES

                Available upon request

James Starbuck
Box 238
Des Moines, Iowa 52621
(319) 535-4791

OBJECTIVE   Marketing/Sales/Management career.

EDUCATION   American Graduate School of International Management, Glendale, AZ
Master of International Management, May, 1982
Concentration: Marketing with emphasis on Asian and Latin American
markets.

San Diego State University, San Diego, CA
Master of Arts program, General Psychology, completed one semester
in good standing, fall, 1980

Drake University, Des Moines, IA
Bachelor of Arts, May, 1980, GPA 3.7
Majors: Psychology, English Literature

Undergraduate Assistant, psychology department, spring, 1980.
- Designed research of inter/intra group cooperation.
- Communicated research proposals to seven public and private
  organizations.
- Enlarged scale of research proposals by incorporating with
  city-wide Cancer Society fund-raiser.
- Aided in arrangement of publicity.

Financed part of undergraduate and 100% of graduate education.

EXPERIENCE   NIEDERNEISEN RFB, Niederneisen, West Germany. October 1982-May 1983.
- Import/Export of tires.
- No. 2 man involved in all facets of operation.
- Suppliers & customers worldwide.

SELF-EMPLOYED, Landscaping Business, Muscatine, IA. Summer, 1980,
Spring, 1981.
- Marketed own services.
- Completed all jobs on or ahead of schedule.
- Received follow-up job offers.

AMALGAMATED TRUCKING CO., Rock Island, IL. Summers, 1977-79.
- Processed shipping documents.
- Transferred $10-40 thousand worth of freight daily.
- Identified and corrected freight transfer problems.
- Trained five new men.
- Operated heavy machinery.
- Received high evaluations from superiors.

J. HENSON CO., Muscatine, IA. Summer, 1976.
- Performed general factory duties.
- Handled hazardous acid materials.

FOREIGN   Foreign study program in Oxford, England for six months.
EXPERIENCE   Center for Bilingual Multicultural Studies, Cuernavaca, Morelos, Mexico.
Extensive travel througout Europe, Asia, and Mexico.

LANGUAGE   Proficiency in Spanish, working knowledge of German.

References available upon request.

CAROL BYRNES
73 Jay Drive
Paramus, New Jersey 08034
(201) 688-3398

MARKETING
Offering a solid background of business experience in marketing, advertising merchandising, management, sales, public relations, accounting procedures. Emphasis on communications and organizational abilities.

EMPLOYMENT RECORD
1980-Present   Mills Products
                                      New York, New York 10001

SHOWROOM SALES SUPERVISOR
Responsibilities include coordinating programs with all major New York retail buying offices; establishing national programs with house key accounts; attending national associations to maintain professional contacts; displaying and reviewing retail line with all customers; acting as liaison between retail accounts and sales persons.

1978-1980   O'Meara's
                                      Paramus, New Jersey 07652

ASSISTANT MANAGER
Supervision of sales staff, fashion coordinating, purchasing, inventory, market projections, consumer research, trend forecasting, advertising, display, sales, prestigious designer womenswear. Modeling.

1979   Dr. John Berger
                                      Department of Economics
                                      Fairleigh Dickinson University

RESEARCH ADJUNCT
Research and correlation of materials, supervision sales and publication reports on women in the contemporary labor force.

1976-1978   Santini Brothers
                                      Paramus, New Jersey 05581

SALES/MERCHANDISING COORDINATOR
Duties included buying, coordinating merchandising principles, standardizing sales procedures, advertising, merchandising multi-unit soft and hard goods specialty store.

EDUCATION   B.S. Business Management
                                      1980, Fairleigh Dickinson University
                                      Honor Society

                                      Presently attending M.B.A. Program
                                      at Fairleigh Dickinson University

PERSONAL DATA
Excellent references furnished upon request. Willing to travel. Hobbies include: Skiing, water sports, art, literature, music, riding, fashion and jewelry design, crafts, gourmet cooking.

MERCEDES BENSON
48 Bayview Road
Sausalito, CA 21360
(812) 328-1925

Professional Experience

July 1977 - July 1980

Sales Promotion Manager
Playtime Corp.

Full involvement in initiation of merchandising display programs
as well as various new product line promotions. Coordinating as
well as conducting full product line presentations to domestic
and international accounts. Product testing. Handled movement
of all printed as well as audiovisual advertising materials to
accounts. Supervised print production of sales promotion brochures, catalogs and sell sheets, both color and black and white,
from preliminary layout through final production. Proofing catalog copy for all legal compliances. Conferred with product and
marketing managers on package design and writing of instruction
sheets. Heavy involvement in preparation of Toy Fair.

February 1966 - May 1977

Executive Secretary
Brokerage: Retail/Institutional Sales

Active in all phases of sales and account management. Assisted
in working of both retail and institutional accounts. Handled
all back office problems and general maintenance of accounts.
Heavy client contact.

Companies worked for include: Mercer Dodge (defunct), Brooks &
Sons, Dillard Inc. (defunct), Levering Securities.

June 1965 - January 1966

Legal Secretary
(General Law)

Heavy typing and steno. Preparation of affidavits and all
correspondence. Setting appointments.

Education   California Institute of Finance
                Studied all aspects of brokerage account management.

                Kingsborough Community College
                One year - studied finance.

Languages   Knowledge of Spanish.

Hobbies   Reading

References   Furnished upon request.

Pedro Bassanta
298 101st Street
College Point, New York 11356
(212) 258-3931

CAREER OBJECTIVE

Continued growth in the area of Customer Service and Purchasing with an opportunity to progress with a sound company.

EXPERIENCE

October, 1981 - December, 1982
Bumblebee Sportswear, Inc., 600 Seventh Avenue, New York, New York. Customer Service Representative.

Showroom sales representative responsible for presenting current designer line to buyers of major department stores and specialty shops. Maintained production and quality control records in addition to administrative tasks. Thoroughly familiar with CRT. Operated ITT Computer for purpose of shipping, fabric availability, seasonal dollar amounts and costs.

February, 1981 - September, 1981
Pinstripe Brothers Shirt Company, 701 Broadway, New York, New York. Customer Service Representative.

Showroom sales representative and liaison with major department store buyers. Maintained perpetual inventory control records. Responsible for a number of clerical functions such as fabric pricing and billing.

September, 1979 - February, 1981
Seoul Bank of New York, 308 Madison Avenue, New York, New York. Customer Service Department.

Responsible for price quotations, answering inquiries related to credit letters, purchase order expediting. Strong mathematical skills were necessary.

November, 1978 - June, 1979
Windons, Inc., 32-36 40th Avenue, Long Island City, New York.

Responsible for handling customer daily inquiries, generating price quotations, maintaining inventory records.

EDUCATION

Bronx School of Science, Bronx, New York. Graduated in 1979.
St. Anne Grammar School.

PETER MISHKIN

208 Old Castle Road
New Canaan, Connecticut 06132
(203) 566-4093

CAREER OBJECTIVE To work as a sales representative in an industrial firm with the opportunity to advance into sales management.

WORK EXPERIENCE EXECUTIVE OFFICE SYSTEMS INC., Greenwich, Ct.
2/82-8/82 - Marketing Representative

Responsible for the sale of photocopiers, supplies and service. Dealt with high-level management in demonstrating and closing orders. Generated sales through canvassing. Acted as customer service representative. Top salesman two out of six months.

MTC BUSINESS PRODUCTS, Norwalk, Ct.
11/81-2/82 - Marketing Representative

Responsible for the sale of photocopiers. Developed territory through establishment of accounts. Top salesman two out of four months. Was recruited to Executive by former manager, who had left a month earlier.

Summers 1979, 1980 - Miro Painting Co., Darien, Ct.
    Assistant crew leader for large, professional company.
Summer 1978 - window washer for self-started residential
    business.

EDUCATION MIAMI UNIVERSITY, Oxford, Ohio, School of Business Administration. Bachelor of Science degree in Marketing Management, May 1981.

HONORS AND
ACTIVITIES
Dean's List - Fall Semester 1980.
Listed in "Who's Who in American High School Students."
American Marketing Association - Publicity Committee.
Sigma Chi Fraternity.
Participated in several intramural sports and captained
    several teams.

REFERENCES Available upon request.

Eric Leary
63 96 Street
St. Paul, Minnesota 55101
(612) 459-2240

CAREER OBJECTIVE: Position in sales or marketing which enables me
to combine my managerial experience with my
proven ability to successfully plan, present and
close a sale.

EDUCATION: Bachelor of Science, Marketing, St. John's
University, Jamaica, New York (May 1978).
Accounting and management minor.

EXPERIENCE: February 1980-present
Sales Representative
Best Company-Foodservice Division
23 Patterson Avenue
Patterson, New Jersey

Territory consists of wholesale distributors and
large chains. Achieved forty per cent real growth
in territory since taking over. Number one sales
representative regionally in attainment versus
target for three sales periods in a row.

Sold in truckload quantities Best label products
and sales agency (other label) products. Performed end-user work with distributor salesmen to
replace competitive product, develop new product
growth. Designed and implemented promotional
activities (direct mailings, in-house sales contests, promotions) to spur movement of product,
increase inventory turns.

June 1978-January 1980
Foodservice Director
Northern Hospital
Dali Food Service

Department head of dietary department. Supervised
dietitians, other managers and dietary workers.
Responsible for budgets, profit/loss statements,
purchasing and compliance with regulatory
commission's standards.

REFERENCES   Will be furnished upon request.

Carl Rohrer, 84-38 145th St., Kew Gardens, N.Y. 11412
212-847-6891

OBJECTIVE: Sales Management

EXPERIENCE: <u>DISTRICT MANAGER</u>: Northwestern Academy

<u>Duties</u>: In charge of 15-20 sales representatives to
interview prospective students for courses in Fashion
Merchandising and Airline/Travel. Hiring, Training,
and Motivating. Advertising, Budgets, Sales Projections. Developed various marketing concepts.

Accomplishments:
- Helped develop an incentive bonus program.
- Implemented complete internal control for follow-up
  procedures of sales force.
- Developed lead procurement program. Results: Increase
  of lead conversion.
- Took over the New Jersey territory and increased sales
  within 6 months.

<u>ACCOUNT EXECUTIVE</u>: Entertainment Associates, Inc.

<u>Duties</u>: Entertainment consulting firm which would marry
management problem solving with artistic expertise.
Used our unique dual role as promotional architects and
consultants to assist institutions who sought promotion
through travel events.

Accomplishments:
- Personally supervised each event, providing everything
  from on-the-spot production to insurance.
- Arranged press conferences, distributed press kits.
- Held press conferences and interviews with performers
  to generate publicity.

<u>SALES CONSULTANT</u>: Global Tours, Inc.

<u>Duties</u>: Wholesale tour company devoted to villa sales
in Jamaica and condominium sales to destinations throughout the Caribbean.

Accomplishments:
- Developed a program for major corporations.
- Ranked Number One in sales.
- Developed various travel groups.

EDUCATION: <u>BBA Accounting, Baruch College, 1974</u>
Institute of Finance, courses in the Stock Exchange.
Colorado State College, courses in Computer Programming.

MILITARY: Finance Specialist 1966-1968, Honorable Discharge.

Marshall Keaton
21 Bramleigh Road
Clementon, NJ 08034
(609) 446-4841

OBJECTIVE: An entry-level position in Marketing or Business Management
                    that provides long-range opportunities for advancement.

EXPERIENCE:

1981 - Present   Databank, Inc., Englishtown, NJ

                    Marketing Representative - Contact businesses in Monmouth,
                    Ocean and Middlesex counties to perform payroll and accounts
                    receivable. Prepare display advertising and brochures.
                    Able to enter data records on the Vector Graphic Computer.
                    Tripled business accounts served since joining this company.

1979 - 1980   Stereo Systems Unlimited, Berlin, NJ

                    Partner, Stereo Equipment Sales - Prepared catalogs, price
                    listings and advertising for stereo equipment products sold
                    on six college campuses in New Jersey, Pennsylvania and
                    Connecticut. Marketed five major product lines purchased
                    through distributors. Maintained sales and accounting
                    records and hired and trained sales representatives.

1976 - 1979   ARA Food Services, Jackson, NJ

                    Assistant Manager, Food Department - Supervised 12 employees
                    responsible for the delivery and setup of beverage containers
                    at service locations throughout the area. Scheduled staff,
                    maintained adequate inventory and performed machine repair
                    services on beverage equipment.

EDUCATION:

1978 - 1982   Glassboro State College, Glassboro, NJ. Bachelor of Arts
                    in Communications and Advertising with a concentration in
                    Marketing.

REFERENCES:

                    References are available upon request.

Bernard N. Simon

620 Norfolk Street
Hackensack, N.J. 07601
(201) 487-4841

OCCUPATIONAL OBJECTIVE: A growth opportunity which affords maximum
utilization of marketing and sales abilities.

EMPLOYMENT

BINGHAM DIVISION OF COSMO INDUSTRIES, INC. MOORESTOWN, N.J. October 1980 -
Present

Hired as territory representative to sell pressure sensitive labels. After
seven months, promoted to cosmetic account manager calling on most major
cosmetic companies in the New York Metropolitan area.

JOHN BRANN PHOTOGRAPHY NEW YORK, N.Y. November 1979 - October 1980

Represented two commercial photographers in new and old account management.
Sales volume was obtained by cold canvassing for new business. Accounts
maintained were Pierre Cardin Fashions, Coty Division of Pfizer, and Hearst
and Fairchild Publications.

BERRINGER CORPORATION PRINCETON, N.J. June 1979 - November 1979

Assisted the manager of market research in all ongoing department activities.
Interacted with all departments in analysis of sales training program and
dealer development organization. Responsibilities included coordinating
research studies, visiting dealers, and innovating ideas for future projects.

EDUCATION

The Pennsylvania State University
Bachelor of Science, May 1979

Graduate Courses: Fairleigh Dickinson University
MBA Marketing Program

HONORS AND ACTIVITIES

Lambda Sigma Society - National Sophomore Honorary
National Forensic Society
Certified in CPR
Dean's List
Patton Accelerator Club - 110% Quota 1981

PERSONAL: Willing to Travel
Fluent in Spanish

REFERENCES WILL BE FURNISHED UPON REQUEST

Robert Cohn
45-28 186th Street
Bayside, New York 12321
(212) 542-4063

_____

EMPLOYMENT

May 1975 to Present   Litholine Press
                           New York City, New York

                           Purchasing Agent
                           Supervised purchasing of chemicals
                           needed for machines; established
                           leads for prospective customer sales.

February 1973 to
May 1975   Quality Press Products
                           Maspeth, New York

                           Sales Representative
                           Sales representative for line of
                           printing chemicals and supplies.

April 1970 to
February 1973   Swiss Machine Co.
                           Lynnbrook, New York

                           Machinist Apprentice
                           Operated mills and Turret Lathes;
                           inspected parts. Use of micrometer,
                           caliper, Rockwell hardness scale.

EDUCATION   Pioneer Marine School - 1970
                           New York, New York
                           Major: In-Board Mechanics

                           Bohrs Technical School - 1976
                           Pittsburgh, Pennsylvania
                           Major: V.I.P. Operator

                           Queens College - 1972
                           Queens, New York
                           Major: Liberal Arts

REFERENCES   Furnished upon request

David Bernstein
28 Vancouver Lane
Ithaca, New York 11283   Tel: 212-861-3020

Career Objectives:
        A position leading to sales/marketing management.

Education:
        Cornell University: Graduated May 1979 with B.S. in Business Manage-
        ment and Marketing. Curriculum included a strong background in
        Marketing and Marketing Management, Financial Management, Accounting,
        Interpersonal Communication, Personnel Management, Labor Relations,
        Economic Theory, Computer Science and Business Math.

Experience:
Nov. 1979-   Vincent and Joseph's Department Store
Jan. 1980

Christmas Merchandising Assistant
°Assisted Buyer in stockwork, inventory control, merchandise transfers,
 returns to vendors, price changes and journal entries.
°Aided in supervision of cashiers and stockpersons. Acted in floor
 sales and other customer transactions.
°Responsible for informing the Buyer of customer preferences as indicated
 through observations and discussions with customers on sales floor.

May 1979-   Financial Systems Corporation
Sept. 1979

System Operator, Programmer-Analyst Trainee
°Operated IBM System 34. Experienced in RPG II, PL/1, and Fortran.
°Responsibility for client contact and correspondence, account manage-
 ment, preparation of proposals and billing.
°Aided in supervision of computer operators and data entries at major
 client, H.A. Lothrop, Customs House Broker.
°Programs included A/R, A/P, updating of customer and vendor files and
 all required customs forms.

Apr. 1974-   A & B Corporation
Aug. 1978
(During   Administrative Assistant
  all   °Responsible for the daily operations of a small firm involved in
school   consulting and sales of data processing equipment and accessories
recesses)   (for IBM automatic typewriters and Mag Card Units).
            °Duties included retail shipping and receiving, inventory control,
             bookkeeping, typing, mail and telephone correspondence, and organ-
             ization of files and mailing lists.

Activities and Organizations:
        °Vice-President of Association for the Help of Retarded Children -
         Ithaca Explorer Group.
        °House Manager and member of Sigma Pi Fraternity, Mu Chapter -
         Responsible for the care of a large house, delegation of work and
         supervision of 60+ members.
        °Photography Editor of yearbook staff.
        °Vice-President and Treasurer of Cornell University Weightlifting Club.
         Responsible for control of funds and equipment purchases for 150+ members.
        °Member Cornell University Track Team.

THE COVER LETTER

Whenever you send your resume to someone whom you haven't met, it should be accompanied by a cover letter. A cover letter, along with your resume, is a marketing tool. A cover letter is also a guide to the information you will cover in greater detail in your resume. It should direct the reader to those areas of your resume that you want highlighted, and it should explain how you can answer the employer's needs.

As with the resume, a cover letter should be an attention-getter. You must make the prospective employer want to read it and the enclosed resume. And it should always be written with your immediate goal in mind: to secure an interview.

Unlike a resume, which is targeted to a broad audience, the cover letter should be as specific as possible. To be most effective, it should be written for a specific individual and must deal with his needs and with the details of the position for which you are applying. If you are sending out scores of resumes, it may take weeks to write individual letters to each prospective employer. The best approach is to develop two or three basic letters that are appropriate to different groups of employers. Put these letters on a word processor (if you can) so that each letter will be individually typed with the recipient's name and address. The companies from which you think you have the best chance of getting a job offer, or that you want to work for most, should be reserved for individual treatment. Your contact information should always appear in your resume, but include it in your cover letter as well. Sometimes it is helpful to identify your most recent job title. But be careful. This could be a good idea if you are applying for work in the same field, but if you are switching fields, it could prejudice an employer against you.

A good cover letter answers five basic questions:

1. To whom is the resume addressed?
2. Who are you?
3. Why are you sending the resume?
4. What do you have to offer this particular employer?
5. What do you propose to do next?

To Whom the Resume is Addressed. It is always best to send your resume to a specific person, if possible. In the cover letter, using a standard business letter format, make sure you have the individual's correct name, title, company and address.

Who You Are. Who you are means your name, address and telephone number, at work and at home, or include any special message number. If you are presently working and want responses handled discreetly, mention this.

Why You Are Sending a Resume. Tell the reader why you are sending this cover letter and resume, and mention if you were referred by a mutual friend or by a professional acquaintance. If you are sending the letter unsolicited, indicate why you have contacted this company specifically, how you have evaluated their needs, or how you think you can contribute to their operation. If you are responding to an advertisement, begin the letter by saying where you saw the ad and which position you are applying for.

What You Have to Offer. What you have to offer this employer is the most important part in your cover letter. You must indicate the needs of *this particular employer*, and why you are the person to answer those needs. You will want to amplify those talents and skills that are most important to this employer, and leave out those attributes that are irrelevant. For example, if you are applying to a French company doing business in the United States, this is not the time to point out that you were a hockey star in high school. This is the time to mention that you speak and write French fluently, that you have studied in Paris, and that you have experience translating business documents from French into English.

What Next. What do you propose to do next? In some way, you must follow up on every cover letter that you write. If you have the name of the company or firm, indicate to the employer that you will telephone him once he has received the letter. If you are responding to a blind ad in a newspaper (no company name or telephone number—just a post office box provided), indicate that you will await a response.

Style and Format

As in every aspect of your job campaign, content is not enough. Style is also crucial. A cover letter should not usually be longer than one page. It should be typed, single spaced, with fairly wide margins, on a quality stock. If you can, use the paper that matches your resume and envelopes. Your cover letter must be letter perfect: absolutely no typographical errors, no misspellings, no smudges, etc. Remember, your cover letter is part of your self-advertisement, a surrogate for yourself. A careless cover letter implies to the reader that you are a careless person. It will make the reader wonder why a person who pays so little attention to his letter will care any more about a job. A company may receive thousands of cover letters each year. You want yours to be special. You must convince the reader that he or she wants to interview you.

Your cover letter also needs a "hook": a single sentence or phrase that highlights your expertise and that sells the reader on you. (See the sample cover letters in this chapter.) If you are sending an unsolicited cover letter, put your hook in the very first sentence. If you are answering an ad, identify the particular ad (you might even quote it) and the newspaper in which it first appeared. Then use your hook.

Finally, your cover letter must be crisply written and easy to read. Keep the sentences concise. Keep thoughts organized by paragraph. Once you have piqued the reader's interest, your next step will be to follow up.

Following Up

In following up on your mail campaign, time is of the essence. A cover letter is "hot" when first received, but cools off quickly. Your cover letter should reach a company two to four days after you have mailed it. So time your follow-up campaign correctly. Try to contact the recipient the same day, or the day after, it crosses his desk.

Follow up on a cover letter with a telephone call. If you are applying to an out-of-town firm, invest in a long-distance call. Once you have gotten your potential employer on the phone, remember the aim of this whole process: to get an interview. Identify yourself, and ask if your letter has been read. If the employer has been swamped with applications, he might say he is too busy to talk; if so, be polite, but assertive and ask when would be a better time to call back. Often, you will be told that your letter was passed on to someone else; find out who that person is. Then, when you call him, say that you spoke to someone else previously, and that you were directed to his office.

Try to schedule an interview during your conversation. If you are told that the company is no longer hiring, try to garner some more information about anticipated future hirings or about other departments which might need help. Again, be polite but persistent.

If you are told that you are not right for the job, try to ascertain why. Perhaps the employer will explain what you could do to improve your credentials or could suggest other places where you might apply.

Whatever happens during your follow-up call, don't be discouraged. Part of marketing anything is dealing with rejections. The more follow-up calls you make, though, the better you'll become at it, and the more the law of averages will work for you.

Keep accurate records of every letter and resume you mail, and every phone call you make. Either keep a carbon of your cover letter, or use an index card with the company's name, address, and phone number. On each card or letter, jot down when you wrote and telephoned, and to whom you spoke. Also note what the response was: Was the job filled? Should you call back in a month? Keep a "tickler file" of this information. It could also be invaluable for you to maintain your contacts for future job searches.

Finally, consider sending a thank-you note to everyone you spoke to or who answered your cover letter. It is noteworthy how few people use this simple technique, and how effective it is for those who do. Whether or not you get this job, a thank-you note leaves a lasting impression. It tells the recipient that you are a thoughtful person, and that you care enough to take the time to be appreciative.

Sample of a cover letter sent on the job seeker's own initiative.

1609 West 100th Place
Chicago, Illinois 60643
January 2, 198___

Mr. Randolph Western
Rogers Business Publications
One Rogers Plaza
New York, N.Y. 10017

Dear Mr. Western:

As an achievement-oriented sales representative with over two years of successful experience in industrial publications, I believe I have much to offer Rogers Business Publications.

I have enjoyed several promotions and am now handling an expanded territory. Prior to my current sales position, I have worked in two industries for which you publish trade magazines. As a customer service representative for an insurance claims department, I gained an in-depth knowledge of the organization; as a part-time sales rep handling auto parts, I became thoroughly familiar with the automotive parts industry, including new car dealers and body shops.

Enclosed please find my resume. I'll be in touch with you shortly to arrange a mutually convenient time for us to meet.

Sincerely,

Gary Owens

Encl.

Sample of a cover letter sent in response to an ad.

James P. Phelps
315 W. 195th St.
New York, NY 10025
(212) 866-5636
June 1, 198—

Compu-National Corporation
1230 Avenue of the Americas
Suite 1212
New York, NY 10016

Attention: Ms. Wilhelmina Brown

Dear Ms. Brown:

In response to your ad for a Sales Trainee appearing in *The New York Times* on June 1, I enclose my resume.

My record of success as a commissioned retail store sales representative during the summers plus my knowledge of data processing make me a very strong candidate for the position you advertised.

I am a very energetic and achievement-oriented individual with a flair for dealing with others. While in college, for example, I founded the Computer Club and was twice elected president.

I would very much like to arrange a mutually convenient time to meet with you. I look forward to hearing from you soon.

Sincerely yours,

James P. Phelps

DEVELOPING YOUR SELF-MARKETING CAMPAIGN

Right at this moment there are probably several available (or soon-to-be available) jobs that you would love to have and that would love to have you. Equipped with the best job-getting tools, your resume, your skills and experience, and you, you are ready to go out there and campaign. But you will have to find out about open positions first.

There are two basic ways of finding out about open jobs. You can let them find you by answering want ads and by applying to employment services; or you can find them by applying unsolicited to companies, using hidden job-hunting techniques and by advertising for employers. The most important ingredient in mounting a successful self-marketing strategy is thoroughness. Do your research, pursue every opportunity and do not forget to follow up on each effort. Use all the methods for job finding. Do not rely on just one. You should be as thorough about looking for a job as you will be on one. It is up to you.

Want Ads

The most common place to find help-wanted ads is in your daily and Sunday newspapers. *The Wall Street Journal* and *The New York Times* are musts, no matter where you live or want to work. Read these ads carefully and comprehensively. Do not only look under "Sales and Marketing." Scan all appropriate listings, including "college grad," if appropriate, or "administrative assistant" or "management trainee." If you are particularly interested in banking, finance, publishing, advertising, or real estate, read those listings, too. And do not confine your reading to daily newspapers. Read any trade magazines and newspapers in your area of interest. (For more information, see our section on directories.)

Help-wanted ads do not only appear in newspapers and magazines. Many businesses post job openings on their bulletin boards or in their newsletters. University placement offices are also a good source for job information. If you are not associated with a school, ask a friend who can check for you.

There are a few things about help-wanted ads appearing in newspapers and trade publications that you should know. Some ads list the name or title of a person or company to contact. Many others don't; these ads are called "blind" ads and only give a post office box, usually in care of the publication, to which you are asked to send a resume and cover letter. The organization placing an ad in a newspaper or magazine may be the employer or a middle person, an employment agency. You can only know for sure if the ad isn't "blind."

If you are currently working, be wary of answering completely blind ads. The job advertised might be an excellent position—but it could also be for your own employer!

WHEN TO ANSWER ADS

Whenever you answer want ads, promptness is essential. Employers cannot wait weeks for every response to come in before filling a position. Often they are in a hurry to find someone and will hire one of the first qualified applicants that they see. Also, promptness in answering a job ad is indicative of promptness at work. Time is also of the essence when you consider the mechanics of placing an ad. The help-wanted notice you see on Sunday could have been placed on Wednesday morning, in order to meet the newspaper's deadline. That means the ad was probably written on Monday or Tuesday—almost a week before you will read it. So it is quite possible, especially if it is an agency ad, that the job was or was about to be filled before you even read about it!

HOW TO ANSWER ADS

There are three ways you can respond to an advertisement: in person, by telephone, or by mail. Of the three, the first is often best. Visit the offices of the firm that has advertised at the first opportunity, dressed for an interview, with your resume prepared. Tell the receptionist that you are there in response to the ad, and ask if you could speak to someone about the job in order to set up an interview. If you are fortunate, you might land an interview on the spot. If no one is available, leave your resume and complete an application for the position. Whether or not you are able to speak with someone, the fact that you appeared in person will leave a positive impression with your prospective employer.

If you are unable to respond to the ad in person, telephone the firm *as soon as you see the ad.* Again, explain your interest in the job and ask to speak with someone about it. Often telephone calls are used to screen potential employees from those applicants who are clearly unsuited for the job. Therefore, be prepared to sell yourself over the phone. Know what to say and how to say it: why you are interested in the job, what your experience has been, and what your current employment status is. Have your resume ready to send if the firm asks to see it.

If you are unable to answer the ad in person or to telephone, answer the ad promptly, by mail. Once again, you must have your resume prepared in advance. You will probably be too late if you wait to have it written and printed after you see the job advertised. Always include a well-written cover letter, explaining your interest in the position and your qualifications.

Hidden Job Market Tip

As we mentioned, you should scour the classified ads in the newspaper for every position that interests you regardless of job title. If you are unsure about a specific job, you might apply for it anyway. You might be pleasantly surprised. And it is better to turn down an offer for a job that you did not want, than to miss a chance at a job you might have wanted had you only applied for it.

There will be many ads for jobs you would like to have but for which you are not or do not feel fully qualified. A company might, for example, ask for two or three years experience when you have only three months. Or, you may have training or related experience, but not what is specifically asked for. You should apply for such jobs anyway; you have nothing to lose and you can only stand to gain. Minimum qualifications in employment ads are fairly arbitrary. The employer wants people who can do the job. It is often anyone's guess as to just how much experience is enough. It is not usually the quantity of experience but the quality that really makes the difference. If you have had three months of experience, you might have as much knowledge as someone with six months, a year or more. Often, the level of knowledge is not the most important factor. The most important factors may be how quickly you can learn, your talent, your professionalism, your energy, and your enthusiasm.

When applying for such jobs, you will have to stress your relevant experience, focusing on "quality not quantity," your learning ability, and all those special aspects of your personality that make you someone who the employer should at least meet.

A special variation of this is to knowingly respond to an ad for a position well above the one you are seeking. If an ad seeks a manager for a department, you may not have the qualifications for the job, but you may have enough experience to qualify for a position as that manager's assistant.

Even if you do not directly respond to help-wanted ads for managers, supervisors or other high-level positions, the ads are worth reading. They could indicate that a firm or department is growing. If a company is looking for managers in marketing, it could be that it is also hiring, or planning to hire, assistants or other departmental staff.

Cracking the Hidden Job Market

Only a small share of the jobs available in any field get advertised. If you want these unadvertised jobs, you cannot wait for them to find you. You have got to go out and find them.

Put your research skills to work on your job search. The main branch of your public library, or any special business, college, or association library has a wealth of resources to help you crack the hidden job market. The most important of these resources are business and professional directories and periodicals. Using these, you can find the names of potential employers, and begin developing a target list, classifying employers by industry, specializations, size, location and so on.

You will want to get the name of the decision maker in each department in which you would like to work, not just the name of the personnel manager. Try to get the name of the sales manager or director of market research if these areas appeal to you—the higher the better. If you start at the top, the boss may either schedule you for an interview or refer you to someone else who is responsible for hiring. With this "recommendation" of the decision maker behind you, for that is what you will say, you will stand a better chance of getting the interview that you want.

To improve your chances of finding employment, it is best to try to identify firms or companies likely to need new staff. For example, if you want to work for a consumer goods manufacturer, look for one that has launched a new product. The best way to find out about specific companies going through expansion and booms is to read periodicals such as *The Wall Street Journal*, *The New York Times*, and trade publications. Identify those expanding firms, figure out what they need and how you can be of use, and then contact the decision maker.

Networking

A major technique in exploring industries, career possibilities and potential employers is networking. Networking means starting with a contact and using that contact to generate another, or several more contacts. Each of these contacts may in turn put you in touch with others. To begin the network, start with the people who you know who are closest to the field you are interested in. You might start with a relative, a schoolmate, a friend of a friend, a distant business connection, a member or official of an association, a neighbor, or someone you see often on the bus.

Your approach is always to seek advice. You would like your contact to share his experience and knowledge with you as you explore the field. Most people love to talk about their work, what they know. And most people feel good when they are able to help others—as long as it does not involve a commitment on their part. So, do not directly ask your contact for a job; just ask to be pointed in the right direction. If your contact knows of a job, he will be likely to mention it. As you conclude your brief, informal conversation, be sure to thank your contact for his time and for help. Perhaps he also knows of someone else with whom you might speak.

Keep track of all the people with whom you have spoken. A thank-you card may be in order after some meetings, especially if you have spoken with someone through a contact.

It Pays To Advertise

It is not only employers who place ads in the classified section of newspapers. Many job seekers have caught onto the idea and advertise for employers themselves. While it is not a technique you should rely upon exclusively, it could be an excellent complement to other job hunting methods, especially if you consult on a freelance basis. In many papers and specialty publications, such as *Multi-Channel News*, a trade serving the cable TV industry, there are "Employers Wanted" and "Services Offered" sections. Advertising here may land you a permanent position or a consultant's spot with a firm needing your special skills. Advertising may also be a way for a beginner to get started.

Accent the positive: your education, your experience and your accomplishments. If you are available for both permanent positions and for project work, indicate this. Read the employer-wanted ads in other publications to see how effectively written they can be.

A sales manager in the cable TV area might place an ad like this one:

CATV Sales Manager

New & Aftermarket Direct Sales Manager. Solid cable background includes two years Regional Sales Manager for major midwest MSO. Also experience in sales, media advertising, marketing and hiring and training sales force. Position in cable or related industry.

Peter M. Smith
1449 Old Indian Village Road
Lac DuFlambeau, Wisconsin 074321
(715) 588-3686

GETTING THE MOST OUT OF EMPLOYMENT SERVICES

Employment or personnel services can be an invaluable resource for jobholders and job seekers on every level. And a personnel counselor can keep you posted on changes within your field, even if you are not on the job hunting trail.

There are four basic types of employment services: executive recruiters, career consultants, permanent agencies and temporary personnel services. Depending upon who you are and what you want to do, any one of these services might be of help to you.

Most modern employment services (except career consultants) earn their profits only if they have successfully placed job seekers in permanent or temporary positions; and, in most cases, the charges for those services are paid by the company, not by the job seeker.

No employment service places all the applicants it interviews. Similarly, not all job seekers find their jobs through employment services; this is especially true for entry-level and executive-level positions. It might happen that you are sent out on an interview for a temporary position soon after completing the registration process. But you will be wisest if you register with two or three employment services while continuing with your own efforts.

Executive Recruiters

Executive recruiters, sometimes known as "headhunters," usually deal with management positions in the $120,000-$150,000 per year range. Because of the high salaries involved, executive recruiters are not licensed (as are employment agencies). Executive recruiters do just what their name indicates. They recruit executives, or, in this case, sales and marketing professionals with usually several years of experience in the profession. The executive recruitment business is primarily employer-related. That is, the job of the executive recruiter is to find people who are qualified for the positions a client needs to fill, not to find jobs for people.

In return for filling a position, the executive recruiter will receive a fee based on a percentage of the employee's annual compensation. This fee, as high as 35% and ranging from $8,000-$22,000, and as high as $35,000 on executives earning over $100,000, is paid by the employer. In some instances, the executive search firm works on retainer—which means the employers pay a fee to the service just to conduct a search. To conduct a search for a specialist, the executive recruiter may have to spend months and thousands of dollars.

Executive recruiters find the people sought by their client through several methods: advertising, referrals and, most important, headhunting. Executive recruiters do not wait for applicants to come to them, they go out and find the people who are right for the job. This means reading trade publications and making dozens of calls. Some headhunters prefer to work with people who are not actively looking for a position for two reasons. First, because someone who isn't looking has a little more prestige than someone who is. Second, as we indicated, they do not find jobs for people, but people for jobs. So, executive recruiters only like to deal with people who they know are qualified for the kind of positions they have. Before you apply to an executive recruiter in person, call first. Discuss your credentials and interests over the phone. If the recruiter believes you match his needs he'll tell you. If not, maybe he can suggest a route for you to take. In any

event, do not lose heart. What the recruiter does or does not need has no bearing on your skills or worth in the job marketplace.

Suppose you are called at your office by a recruiter; what should you do? The recruiter will try to do four things: interest you; qualify you to see if you are right for the position; have you come in for an interview (where practical) if he believes you are right for the position he has; see if you can recommend others who may be qualified for the position, if you are not qualified or interested.

There is no harm in talking to an executive recruiter. Naturally discretion is required. If you are in a particularly sensitive situation, you can ask for the recruiter's name, firm name, and telephone number, and call him or her back. This is often a good idea when you are unsure of the recruiter's reputability or of whether your own firm is testing the loyalty of its employees (which happens, although not too often). If you cannot talk in the office, you might consider having the recruiter call you at home. If possible, it's best to listen to what the recruiter has to say. Find out about the particular position for which he is recruiting —the salary, duties, growth potential, company and industry. Also, find out what other types of positions the recruiter handles. During this conversation, the recruiter will be trying to find out about you; use this as leverage to get the information you want. In answer to his questions about your skills, experience and desires, be sure to sell yourself—even if you are not currently looking for a job. Next year you might be, or the recruiter may uncover a once-in-a-lifetime job that you'll want him to call you about. If you alienate the recruiter, he may not.

Of course, working with an executive recruiter involves trust. If you do not feel that the chemistry is right between you and the recruiter, politely but firmly tell him that you are not interested in exploring the matter and that you regret that you will be unable to help him in any way whatsoever. But if you do trust the recruiter, you may ask him to keep a weather-eye out for unusual opportunities or you may even be interested in the position about which you were called. If so, be sure that you clearly understand how your resume or credentials will be presented to specific employers. You may request the executive recruiter to contact you for approval before presenting your resume to an employer, or you may give the recruiter a range of companies and positions for which he may freely forward your candidacy. Be sure to specify, in as much detail as possible, the kinds of positions, companies, industries you'd like to work in. Talk freely about duties, responsibilities, compensation, and locale—without unreasonably narrowing your options.

Career Consultants

Career consultants do not as a rule find people jobs. Career consultants help people find out what type of job they want, what type of job they are looking for, and then they help job candidates to best package themselves in preparation. Such services might include working on resume writing, interviewing, job hunting techniques and even salary negotiation.

For this service, the job seeker pays a fee to the career consultant. This fee might be by the hour, by the service, or by a percentage of the job candidate's current or desired salary. In most cases, there is no guarantee that the job candidate will find a job, although some career counselors do offer placement assistance. So, if you are considering going to a career consultant, you may wind up paying a substantial fee whether or not you get a job, or whether or not the career consultant played any part in securing your new position. There is nothing wrong with this as long as you are clear about what you want from the career consultant and about what he is prepared to offer. Review a career consultant's qualifications, inspect his services and ask to speak with previous clients before deciding to sign up.

If you are a sales or marketing professional, you should be able to quickly develop the skills you need to write an excellent resume, interview for a job or negotiate a salary. And so you will most likely not need a career consultant. But, even if you do have these skills, you still might wish to seek a consultant's services for two reasons. First, as a means of prompting yourself to undertake the task of correctly packaging yourself and working on your career skills, just as you might join a health club, even though you could easily exercise regularly on your own. Second, career packaging takes time. If you can't afford the time, or would rather not spend it, you might consider hiring a career consultant.

Employment Agencies

Employment agencies are licensed companies that find permanent positions for people looking for jobs, and, of course, people to fill permanent positions for companies seeking employees. The word "agency" applies only to this type of employment service. Agencies perform this referral service for a fee, which is based on a percentage of the employee's projected first year's compensation. This fee is usually paid by the employer.

To select an employment agency, look in the Yellow Pages, the Sunday classified ad section of the newspaper, and in any specialized trade publications. Select several that seem to have ads in your field of interest and which have the widest selection of jobs of all types.

Register with a few employment services and judge for yourself. You will want the best service from counselors who have your interests most at heart. All things being equal, an agency which pays its counselors on salary, not on commission, may be better. A counselor is then less likely to encourage you to apply for a job for which you wouldn't be satisfied.

Be honest with the agency, even if you have something you think might be negative in your background. The good agency will help you find something positive in it. Also, feel free to discuss the interviews that you have been on, and what you have liked and not liked about specific companies. This will help the agency to avoid duplication of effort and to target the best jobs for you.

Agency Fees. At most modern employment services, the employer pays the fee, you do not. You can easily find out whether an agency is "fee paid" by reviewing their classified ads in the newspaper, by looking in the Yellow Pages, or by making a phone call.

Temporary Personnel Services

Temporary personnel services, not properly called "agencies," earn their profits by "renting out" the services of temporary employees to clients. If you work as a temporary, each job you work on is called an assignment. Although you may be on the same assignment for anywhere from just a few hours to well over a year, you are actually the employee of the temporary service and are paid an hourly wage by the service.

In addition to your salary, the temporary service is also responsible for your social security payments, unemployment compensation insurance and claims, worker's compensation, and disability insurance. And, as the temporary service must cover the cost of marketing, interviewing and placing you on the payroll, the temporary service's "rental" charge is slightly more than your hourly wage. After your salary is paid and all the expenses are covered, temporary services usually earn a very small profit margin.

Why Work Temporary? Working temporary can be a stepping-stone to permanent employment, especially if you are a beginner. If you are working temporary for a company, your position could become permanent —the project you are working on might go on for a long time, or you might impress an employer with your skills, personality and hard work. An office job in a sales or marketing department just might be the "foot in the door" you need. The contacts you make while working temporary can also be an invaluable asset in your continued job search. You might also use temporary work to finance your job search so that you can afford to wait for the right offer. And you can use temporary work to explore different fields or companies first hand.

THE INTERVIEW

Every step on your self-marketing campaign leads to the interview. You are confident, you know who you are, what you want and what you have to offer. You know that the employer has already expressed interest, otherwise you would not be interviewing.

The purpose of the interview is to get a job offer, even if you should decide you do not want the job. You can always turn down an offer, and there is nothing like being offered a job to boost your confidence. To get the offer, you will have to sell yourself. Of course, you will also use the interview to find out whether you want the job. You must balance selling yourself with exploring the company and the position.

The Interview Process

Most successful candidates go through two or three interviews: an initial screening interview by a personnel manager; a second interview with a department head, supervisor or other decision maker; and a final interview where the last details are covered and an offer is extended. Each interview has a different purpose; and you will need a different strategy for each one.

THE FIRST INTERVIEW

Most likely, your first interview will be with someone whose job it is to separate the wheat from the chaff. This person is often a recruiter or personnel manager, and usually not the person for whom you'll be working. He is not likely to be the one to hire you either. Moreover, he will not likely know, or be able to tell you, what the job is really like. You will only find that out from your prospective supervisor and perhaps from the people actually working in that department.

With this in mind, you have only one objective: to get past the screener, to be called back for a second interview with a decision maker. At your first interview, your strategy should be directed primarily towards selling yourself and secondarily towards exploring the job. Listen carefully to each question for clues that will help you sell yourself to the interviewer. You must show interest in the position and in the company.

If the interviewer has not volunteered the information, ask "What can you tell me about the position?" and "What can you tell me about the company?" Do not question the interviewer too persistently about the details. And, always frame a question in a positive way. Do not ask, for example, "Will I have to spend most of the time doing detail work?"

Two topics you should probably avoid bringing up on the first interview are salary and promotability. Do not argue about salary on the first interview. You will probably have a fair idea of the earning potential of the position from the ad you answered or from your personnel counselor. If the interviewer asks what salary you are looking for, it is best to answer indirectly. You might, for example, say something like this: "Finding the right job in which I can make a solid contribution to the company and which makes good use of my skills is really my top priority. I can be somewhat flexible about the salary." If the job is a commission position, then wanting to earn as much as possible is in your favor, provided that the figure you want is possible.

On the first interview, avoid asking about whether the job is promotable. The interviewer may volunteer the information; you, however, want to do a good job on the job for which you were hired, before considering a move. It is acceptable to mention career growth as an objective, but you do not want to give the impression that you are after the *next* position before you become successful in this one.

Finally, do not worry about whether the job seems ideal. Meet the decision maker and learn about the job first. Who knows, if you are well liked, a new position might be created especially for you.

THE SECOND INTERVIEW

If you have been invited back for a second interview, congratulations. It is on this interview that you will really get a chance to sell yourself and to find out in detail what the job involves and what it has to offer.

Usually, the interviewer will ask the first questions. Again, listen for clues. Usually these questions will be about what you have done on previous jobs and what you are looking for. Use each answer unobtrusively to promote yourself. In addition, have the interviewer describe a typical day, in addition to the regular duties and responsibilities, so that you will get a good idea of the balance of work. Also, ask about any unusual circumstances that might come up: special projects, travel, and so on. Ask about the department, the people, and the organization. Ask the employer to describe an ideal candidate for you; you will learn a lot about the job and the employer in this way.

You might ask, as the interview progresses, why the job has become open. Was the previous person promoted? If so, to what position? Is it a new position? If so, how does the employer see the position in relation to the rest of the company? What special problems or challenges does the employer see in successfully establishing the new position? If the previous employee left, ask why.

Discuss salary at the end of the interview, unless of course the interviewer mentions it first. If asked, sidestep the question as we discussed earlier and ask instead what salary range the position offers. Make sure you also ask about all the fringe benefits, bonus plans and the like.

By this time in the interview you should have demonstrated your professionalism, your qualifications and your interest in the position. You should have determined the details of the position and you should also have a clear idea of whether you are interested in exploring the job further or in considering an offer. You will, of course, want to know when the employer is ready to make a decision and when the employer wants the new employee to start.

If you are interested in the position, let the employer know it and also let it be known why you think you will do a top-notch job. Whether you accept an offered position on the spot or whether you ask for time to consider the offer depends upon how much you like the job, how pressed for time the employer is, and where you are in your job search. Never turn down a position on the spot, even if you know you do not want it. You can use the offer as a bargaining position elsewhere, or you may find that the job really looks a lot better after you have considered the alternatives.

THE THIRD INTERVIEW

If you have been asked back for a third interview, you should hope to walk out the door with a job offer. Use the interview to clarify any outstanding details and to convince the interviewer that you are the right one for the position.

Interviewing Techniques

Prepare for every interview before you walk into the office. Review your resume and have all the information about your skills, education and work experience at your fingertips. Research the firm and be sure to develop an in-depth familiarity with its product or specialty and how it stacks up against the competition. Be prepared with answers to tough questions in advance, especially if you have limited experience or if you have left a job because of problems. You may even want to rehearse interviewing with a friend beforehand.

Your attitude is critical at every interview. You will not only be judged by what you answer, but also by how you answer: how you comport yourself and how you articulate your answers. Be friendly and outgoing. Maintain good eye contact and sit upright but relaxed in your chair.

Many interviews begin with small talk. Feel free to chat a little, but do not lose your professional composure or stray from the purpose of the interview. And do not volunteer personal information about your religion, politics, or family. Above all, do not make negative comments about yourself or about a previous job or employer.

Let the interviewer ask the first question, and be a good listener. Take a moment to reflect before you answer. Give concise, well-formulated answers. The length of your responses is not as important as their content.

You control the interview by answering questions and by asking them—not by talking on or by appearing to take control away from the interviewer. Always allow the interviewer to appear to be in command. Consider what is behind the questions the interviewer asks. For example, a question like: "Do you have many outside commitments or family obligations?" might mean: "Can you work overtime or on weekends to meet a deadline or a rush project?" Be prepared to answer honestly, but emphasize your flexibility and dedication. Word your answers to emphasize how your skills can help your prospective employer. After you finish your answer, stop talking! Wait for the interviewer to respond, and gauge his response.

You do not have to wait for the interviewer to ask the right questions. You can steer the conversation the way you want. It is up to you to demonstrate the relevancy of your remarks by tying them to some aspect of the job and by showing how your skills or accomplishments would be beneficial.

IF YOU QUIT OR WERE FIRED

If you quit or were fired from a previous job, you must be prepared to answer an interviewer's questions about this. Of course, you never want to volunteer information about why you left a job, but, if pressed, formulate an answer that puts you in the most favorable light. Consider what you will answer before the interview. Do not respond with an outright lie—the interviewer need only call your previous employer to get his side of the story—but learn to stretch the truth without breaking it.

DRESS

Part of a successful marketing campaign is advertising and promotion. The other part is packaging. The way you dress for an interview is your personal packaging, and it makes a big impression—whether positive or negative—upon your interviewer.

The basic rule should be obvious: always come to an interview well dressed. If you want to be treated as a professional, dress like one. For men, this means a tie and suit, for women, a skirt or dress and blazer.

Dress well for your job interview, but do not over-dress. Leave the evening clothes, flashy jewelry and heavy perfume at home. Think of yourself as an actor auditioning for a role in a play. To get the part, dress for it.

SMOKING

Do not smoke!—even if the interviewer offers you a cigarette.

NEGOTIATING THE SALARY YOU WANT

Negotiating salary is likely to be the most delicate part of your entire job-hunting process. Naturally, you want as much as you can get. To the employer you must present this as wanting to be paid what you are worth. In negotiating salary, you do not want your prospective employer to see you as someone who is self-centered, someone who asks not what he can do for his company, but how much his company will pay him. Yet, if you do not ask for what you are worth, you will not get it. Your personality and expertise are special commodities being purchased by the employer. There are six factors which go into determining what you are worth.

Stated Salary Range. First, there is the salary range as stated by the employer. It is best if the salary is stated in terms of a range; a range shows flexibility. If you bring up the question of salary, ask for a range. If the employer mentions a flat figure, you might test the flexibility by asking "Is that at midpoint?" If yes, then you know that you can negotiate for more! How much more depends upon other factors.

It is the decision maker who usually determines the salary. Sometimes he must work within a company-defined range and cannot go beyond it. But many times the salary range quoted falls comfortably below the company specified ceiling. And many times the ceiling is flexible.

The Salary of the Previous Person in the Job. If you know how much the last person in the job you want made, you might get an indication of how much you can earn; if you are doing the same job, you should be paid as much or a little more. Be careful about asking this. The previous employee may have been making less than you are in your current job.

Your Previous Earnings History. If you are changing jobs within the same field, then your previous earnings history will probably influence the salary offer. If the job will pay as high as $25,000 per year, but you make $15,000 now, it is unlikely that you will be paid $25,000, unless you have an unusual talent or another job offer at that salary.

The standard salary increase within the same field is between $1,000 and $3,000 (sometimes as high as $5,000) for salaries of under $30,000 per year. The higher the salary, the greater the increase for changing jobs. If you want more, you will probably have to negotiate for it and you may also have to negotiate for it if your current salary is already high in respect to the company's range for the position.

We do not recommend taking a job at a salary cut. At the very least, an employer should offer you the same salary that you are making now. But even then, you must be getting something more out of it—experience, opportunity, benefits. If an employer does not think enough of you to pay you what you are worth, or if he says he can't afford to, then you may not be happy in the job. It may not ultimately be for you.

The Going Rate in the Field. The going rate in the field is what other people make in similar positions with similar experience. If the salary quoted for the position is a bit less than the going rate, indicate this to the employer. If the salary that you are asking is higher than the going rate, you will need to be able to show why you deserve it.

What You Can Do for the Company. If you want a hefty increase over your current salary or more than the employer initially seeks to pay, then you have got to demonstrate that you are worth it. Be creative in showing what steps you will take if hired to improve upon what has previously been done in the position. That is worth more money!

How Much Should You Say You Want. You should now have a pretty good idea of what you are worth and what you can get. Your asking price should combine what you think you are worth with what is realistic to ask for. If you think $5,000 more is what you should get, ask for it. Be firm, but do not ask for $10,000 more with the idea that you will settle for $5,000. If you play such games, you will be the loser.

Your strategy should be to try to get the employer to announce what he or she wants first. Then you can come back with what you want and why. If you think you are worth more, hold out for it. If the employer doesn't want to pay you what you ask, find out why.

You might then want some time to think over an offer.

If you feel brave and can afford to risk losing the job, you can ask to think it over and later call back to tell the interviewer that you would really like to accept the job but can only do so at the higher figure. If the employer really wants you, you may get more. If not, you have lost the job. Let's hope, if you lose the job, you will have other and better opportunities. If you do, you will have lost nothing and had a chance to gain.

Choosing Between Jobs

If you are fortunate enough to have received more than one job offer, you will have to choose between them. If the job offers seem similar, getting as much detail about them as possible will be helpful. Try to get a specific daily job description from your prospective employers. Find out how you will actually be spending your work days and who you will spend most of your time working with.

Go back to your list of job objectives, and review them. See how each job meets the goals you have set for yourself. If you are really in a quandary, list the pros and cons of each position on paper. Consider the salaries, but keep in mind that even if your main objective is financial, a job with frequent promotions, salary reviews, and excellent benefits can outweigh one with a higher starting salary.

Whether or not you accept a job offer, write a thank-you note to the people with whom you have interviewed. Few people do this, and it is something an employer will remember. If you are a semi-finalist, it could tip the balance your way. And even if you are not interested in the job, you never know when you will apply at that company or firm again, or to whom your interviewer might speak. Your reputation is one of your greatest assets. Do everything you can to enhance it.

USING DIRECTORIES, PERIODICALS AND REFERENCE BOOKS

Directories and periodicals can help you determine which companies and industries you will want to pursue. They can tell you which companies are expanding or moving—companies that might need your skills. And when you are ready to go on an interview, they are a research tool that will help you prepare in-depth the information that you want.

In addition to researching different companies that could use your skills, it is important to learn all you can about the sales and marketing fields, whether you are a beginner or have been in the field a while.

Reading books, magazines, and newspapers about sales and marketing and about specific industries that interest you is important. You will keep abreast of changes and advances and will see opportunities before they pass you by.

The place to begin your research is with the main or business branch of your local public library. University libraries are also good sources of information. You might look, too, in the Yellow Pages of your telephone book, under libraries and associations, to find additional specialized resources. Reference librarians can help you further. If you want to work for a particular company, try to get a copy of its annual report. Often it is free for the asking, and it is a source of much valuable information. Finally, check the annual subject index of newspapers, magazines, and journals of particular interest as an additional resource.

A few major resources for job hunters are listed below. For more information, see the Appendix, "For Further Reading."

Business and Legal Directories

STANDARD AND POOR'S
Standard and Poor's, New York, NY

Standard and Poor's is a comprehensive listing of U.S. corporations, as well as of some foreign firms. You will find the names and titles of the chief officers for each company, and a description of each company's major products or services. A companion volume focuses on American executives, and includes their educational and work history. The index separates companies according to type of business and geographical location.

There are several ways to use *Standard and Poor's*. Check the geographical index to find the names of companies in your location. The business index tells you what companies are involved in your field of interest.

MILLION DOLLAR DIRECTORY
Dun & Bradstreet, Inc., Parsippany, NJ

This directory, published in three volumes, provides information on over 120,000 U.S. businesses with a net worth over $1,500,000. Volume I lists 49,000 top companies ranked by net worth. The remaining companies are included in Volumes II and III. The directory provides access to companies alphabetically by business name, geographically, and by business classification (SIC codes).

DIRECTORY OF SPECIAL LIBRARIES AND INFORMATION CENTERS
Gale Research Company, Detroit, MI

This three-volume directory is self-described as "a guide to special libraries, research libraries, information centers, archives and data centers maintained by government agencies, business, industry, newspapers, educational institutions, nonprofit organizations and societies in the fields of science, technology, medicine, law, art, religion, history, social sciences and humanistic studies." Volume I is a directory of special libraries and information centers in the United States and Canada. Volume II lists these libraries and centers by geographic location, and Volume III is a New Special Library Supplement.

DIRECTORY OF DIRECTORIES

As the name indicates, this is a reference guide to directories in every business, government and civic field you can imagine.

Other Directories

The number of directories at a good library can be extensive. If you want to dig further, try the following:
Encyclopedia of Associations, Gale Research Co., Detroit, MI
National Trade and Professional Associations, Columbia Books, Inc., Washington, DC.

THE YELLOW PAGES

Do not overlook this old standby as another possible job identification source.

7
Advancing Your Career

NO matter how long or short a time you have been in sales, there are always new ways in which you can improve your career. Many people only give serious consideration to improving their careers when they find they want or need something different. More money, more responsibility, a change of environment. Working towards improving your career should, however, be an ongoing responsibility you owe to yourself, just as doing a good job at work is part of your responsibility to your employer.

Career improvement takes thought, commitment, and work. But it is worth it in terms of the additional satisfaction gained from developing goals and attaining them. It makes the difference between a job and a career!

PROFESSIONAL ADVANCEMENT— WHAT IS IT?

While most people want professional advancement, it is hard to say exactly what it is, as professional advancement may mean different things to different people. Career advancement may be looked at in five different ways: growth and diversity; compensation; increased responsibility; increased recognition; and better working conditions.

Bear in mind that success in one area of advance-ment leads to success in another. Increased recognition often leads to increased responsibility and increased compensation. Excellent performance may lead to increased responsibility and then to greater recognition. Once you have decided what your professional advancement goals are, you'll need to map a strategy for accomplishing them.

What does advancement mean to you? In sales or marketing, career advancement doesn't stop at the door of your company or your present situation. Based on your sales experience, and, in some cases, additional skills you may have or can learn, there are scores of exciting, high-paying alternatives your career can take. Just a few of these alternatives are: starting up your own company, writing on sales topics, designing a sales training course, advancing into sales management or marketing, opening a specialized consulting firm, or working for an industry association.

If you want to advance your career, you may need to improve your effectiveness as a salesperson. This may mean brushing up on your sales techniques and doing more research on your industry. It may mean taking a sales course, either within your company or outside. Anything you can do to upgrade your performance will help you move up—whether you want to move up within your company or to change to another company.

If you're thinking of switching companies, look at your current situation and then look at the next rung up the ladder. Does that "rung" exist at the company you'd like to switch to? If it's a company that's enjoying rapid growth, they may not yet have gotten around to establishing that job category. But *you* may be able to sell them on creating it.

When considering a likely promotional opportunity, you may not want to focus exclusively on sales. Remember, sales experience is regarded as excellent background for many kinds of jobs within an organization. For example, people skilled and experienced in sales can consider management positions—either on the sales side or the purchasing side. Or they can move into marketing and related areas such as advertising and public relations.

Have you considered going on for an advanced degree such as an MBA? Your company may have a tuition-refund program that would greatly ease the financial burden. If your company does not offer a tuition-refund program, that's something to look for when you do decide to make a switch.

Do you want to stay in your industry or do you want to move to a new one? Or to a related industry? To a company that's just getting started or to one that's just maturing? By reading publications such as *The Wall Street Journal* and *Business Week*, along with specific industry publications, you can find out where the growth areas are in the economy—and what the long-term trends are.

Should you stay in one industry for a long time? If you don't want to be pigeonholed, you should take time to evaluate your industry—and its prospects. Will your industry last as long as you do? Does your industry have the longevity to see you through your career?

If you're switching companies, or switching fields, don't forget that you've built something where you are—a client base, a knowledge base, a track record. When deciding whether to make a switch, you have to consider what you have to lose—and what you have to gain. Any career changes should be made on careful reflection, not on impulse.

Also, when switching, you should note whether there is a non-compete clause in your contract? Such a clause may impede you from transferring to a competing company. However, you should check with a lawyer. Some restrictive contracts are not as enforceable as they seem.

Below is a discussion of some of the most common interpretations of the meaning of career advancement. Add your own ideas to this list under each category and then decide what's most important to you. Do not

be modest or conservative—be daring; however, don't ask for more than you really want. Then, using the strategies outlined in the "Job Finding Primer" (chapter 6) identify those positions that will provide you with the career satisfactions you seek.

Growth

Growth for salespeople means more than the acquisition of a national account or promotion to a more prestigious job title, though these are usually important indicators. It also means developing such skills as how to deal with clients or superiors; how to supervise other salespeople, how to budget time better, or how to improve self-discipline. This may mean an increased sense of personal satisfaction in what you do.

Diversity means expanding your range of sales expertise, either by learning new specialties, developing new applications or customer bases for a product or service, or increasing your knowledge in a given area. Career growth and diversity also mean learning what your weaknesses are by self-examination or through feedback from someone you respect—and working to strengthen those areas.

Compensation

Of course, money is important—both for what it can buy and as a psychological boost, an acknowledgment that you are valued. Salary may be a prime objective for you, but don't make it a single-minded pursuit. And compensation, of course, involves more than take-home pay; it also includes medical and dental benefits; pension plans; tuition refunds; profit sharing; and vacation time. Consider these benefits, along with salary, as an entire compensation package.

If you seek additional compensation, you have three options: to stay where you are and ask for a raise, to stay in the profession but apply to other firms, or to leave sales/marketing for another field. If you decide to leave your current job, your course of action is pretty clear: find the job that offers what you want. But assuming you would like to continue where you are, there are several ways you can increase your earnings.

First, have a salary goal in mind. Don't undersell yourself, but at the same time be realistic. Read ads and talk to your colleagues in other firms to learn what the going rate is for someone with your experience. If you approach your manager with an unsupportable request, it is likely to be denied. Once you have done your homework, appproach someone at the firm whom you trust and respect—your supervisor or, if possible, a mentor—and explain why you think you are worth more. Mention what experienced people in your position are earning elsewhere, but also stress your own achievements: your efficiency and expertise, your commitment and work, your contributions beyond the call of duty.

Increased Responsibility

For many sales professionals, increased responsibility is a prime objective. If that is true for you, determine what projects your corporation or firm is involved in that you feel you could take on. Assess your own qualifications. If you have technical or managerial skills that are not being used, find out where or how they might be used.

Using this information, draw up a proposal for increasing your responsibility. Show how the tasks you have in mind tie into your work experience and training. Even more important, show how your increased responsibility can benefit the managers in your firm or department. Almost every employer would like to achieve three goals: a better work product; increased work capacity; increased income for the firm and reduced overhead. Your job is to convince your supervisor that you can accomplish all three.

Recognition

Seeking recognition for your accomplishments is a natural, vital part of career satisfaction. A good employee with a professional attitude often takes on tasks and additional responsibilities beyond the initial job description. To be recognized for these accomplishments, you may have to "toot your own horn."

You can often gain additional recognition within your firm by becoming involved in any special activities such as committee or volunteer work, or by contributing to a company newsletter.

You can also gain recognition outside your office. For example, you might join your local professional sales association, get involved, and perhaps become an officer. You may give lectures at sales meetings and conferences or write articles about your area of expertise or issues in the sales field. Recognition outside the office may be of value to you within the office as well, as your supervisor and others perceive your contribution to the field.

Better Working Conditions

One day you might decide "If only I had a window, I'd be happier." Sometimes, simple things like the office decor, location or overtime can make a big difference. There are probably ways in which your working conditions could be improved. Some of these may only come with a promotion or other recognition,

others might be improved with a little effort on your part—because no one else has given the matter much thought.

DEVELOPING A SUCCESSFUL CAREER PLAN

There are two ingredients essential to advancing a career, an open mind and a plan. An open mind is needed to look at each opportunity freshly, to avoid dismissing avenues of growth on the basis of first impressions or labels, and to venture into a completely different area from what you've been doing or from what you've thought you'd like to do.

Most of all, you will need a plan. Without one, you may receive promotions, or you may happen upon a new career opportunity, but it is not as likely. If you look around you, you may find that there are a number of people with less impressive credentials or talents, but who seem to be a bit farther along in their careers than you. Do they "have all the luck?" There is no discounting the advantages of luck. But equally true, you can make your own luck, and most successful people do. Making your own luck is a matter of having a goal, having a plan—and moving toward that goal continually—however slowly—according to your plan. If you do, you will expose yourself to more opportunities. Of course, the more opportunities the greater the chance the law of averages (or luck) will work in your favor. And, of course, by continually working at improving your career you will probably also be improving your skills and thus your qualifications and capacities for career advancement. While these remarks may seem obvious, it is true that many people, while recognizing their validity, never act on them.

Goal! Plan! Action! One impediment to following these exhortations is that goals often seem so far away. This distance suffused with a touch of wishful thinking often gives career goals an aura of unreality. And so achieving career goals often remains something that we would like to accomplish "someday." Your plan is a bridge across the distance from where you are today to the far-off goals of tomorrow. A successful plan is one which covers the entire distance without any breaks or gaps, without leaving any middle steps out—no matter whether the ultimate goal will take just a few months to achieve, or many years. If you are a field sales representative and wish to become a vice president of sales and marketing, your plan may lead from a promotion to national account sales representative and then to product sales manager, then from an evening MBA program to a position in new product development, and then finally to vice president of sales/marketing.

The above example represents just one possible route to take. For every goal there are usually many possible routes. You might be able to reach your goal within your company or by switching from company to company, or from industry to industry. Sit down and list, step by step, the various routes through which you can attain your distant career goals. How many alternative paths can you draw —however wild? Next, develop some alternative goals that provide you with the income and sense of achievement you desire. How many alternative goals can you develop? For each of these goals, perform a similar analysis of alternative paths.

In completing this process, you will have sketched the total matrix of *foreseeable*, preferred career advancement paths. This is the world you will most likely inhabit during the course of your career—the totality of career possibilities. Based on this matrix, you can now determine the path most assured of success. The path most likely to be successful is the one whose different way stations are shared by the greatest number of alternative routes. To visualize this, imagine drawing your alternative career plans as separate maps, each on an individual sheet of transparent plastic. Each step on a career advancement path is a town on the way to a major city, your final career goal. Now, overlay the maps. The most common routes are those most likely of success, assuming that all routes are equally difficult or likely. Adjust for the likelihood or difficulty of moving from stage to stage on various alternative career paths, and you will have scientifically developed the career route most likely to succeed.

A CAREER JOURNAL

You have now developed one or more career routes most assured of success. However, you have not developed a plan. A plan is something formal and tangible. To turn these sketches into something more objective, more real and more action-oriented, write them down in a place where they can't be lost or ignored. The best place is a career journal. A career journal is an almost sacred book in which you keep all plans and information relative to your career. For example, you'll note the results of career exercises like Taking Stock Of Yourself and Clarifying Your Objectives, which are outlined in the "Job Finding Primer." In addition, you should keep any information on job descriptions that interest you, including the help-wanted ads. For each job you have plotted along your success path, write down all the duties involved and qualifications required. As you talk with people and read news or trade publications, clip out appropriate articles and keep notes on information relevant to your career. Every time you have a thought or make a resolution which you would like to hold on to, write it down in your career journal. Keep your journal and career plans updated to reflect new wants, changes in opportunity and changes in your circumstances.

As good as your plan may become it still lacks one dimension. That dimension is time! Your action-oriented plan will need a timetable. How long will each step take? How long will you allow each step to take? Establish a cut-off point, a time limit, for each step so that you will know when to call a halt and start off in a new direction. One of the key ingredients to a plan is knowing when to abandon it. Many people stay stuck in one place a long time because they want to stick to their plan or they are afraid to embark in a completely new direction. If you're not getting somewhere, move into a new direction where you can pick up momentum.

The penultimate step in finding your career advancement will be to write out a timetable, starting from where you are today. Write a list of the dates and places where you expect to be according to your plan. Is your plan a realistic one? Block out a timetable at 6-month intervals. Mark off where you will be every six months. The finishing touch will be to plan, on a month-by-month and week-by-week basis, the things you will need to do (both in and out of work) in order to arrive at your six-month destination. For the six-month period in which you are in now, make a checklist of things to do in your career journal. Transfer each day's or week's items to your desk calendar or pocket diary. Now do the things on your list, and then check them off. Each time you accomplish one of the small items on that list, you have been successful. If you only write things down on your daily list that you are capable of performing, you will be successful!

FOUR RESULTS-GETTING CAREER IMPROVEMENT STRATEGIES

Finding a Mentor

Once you have decided upon your career advancement goals, you will need to find ways to accomplish them. It is almost impossible to walk into a management meeting with a surprise request. The best way to achieve your goals within your current company is to get someone to "go to bat" for you.

For an ally, choose someone whom you trust and respect, someone who has some influence and who is sympathetic to your interests and situation. It is best if the individual is your supervisor or someone who already knows you through your work. But, depending upon the situation, your mentor can be someone else, perhaps someone whom you got to know as part of the mentor strategy. In order to plan to meet a mentor, chose an activity, if possible, in which the mentor will have a chance to observe your abilities. Is this individual involved in any "extracurricular" company activities or organization which you can join and participate?

The secret to winning an ally is to be of help to your mentor as you gradually develop a relationship. Show how the goals you want will be helpful to your ally, the firm, or both. Allow your mentor to give you the benefit of his experience. If you phrase your goal in terms of a problem that you would like to have help solving, you will get the best results. Everyone feels good and important if they have helped someone else. Moreover, if your ally has participated in arriving at the solution, he or she will be energetic and positive about putting it into effect.

Changing Jobs

If you'd like a hefty raise and perhaps additional responsibility along with it, you owe it to yourself to think about seeing what else is available. In fact, we recommend that whether or not you're actively looking for a new job, you keep an eye out for what's happening in the marketplace—you may find that most salespeople with your experience are earning more. If so, you've got a good reason to ask for an increase right where you are—or to make a switch. The best way to keep tuned with the marketplace is to watch the help-wanted ads in the papers and to register with an employment counselor or head-hunter at an established agency specializing in sales careers. Your personnel counselor is in touch with hundreds of employers all the time. He or she can tell you about current trends over the phone. You can easily find out whether you're underpaid or underchallenged and what you can do about it.

Simply changing jobs may enable you to increase your income substantially—by several thousand dollars a year. To earn more money, you'll have to do three things: locate the right type of position, package yourself correctly, and negotiate well. Once you're an experienced professional, it's not wise to start mailing out your resume unsolicited. It could get back to your own employer! What's more, if you're a busy, hard-working professional, you won't be able to take the time out really needed to conduct a full-scale search on your own. A personnel counselor can do this for you.

Once you find a prospective employer who really seems to want you, then you'll be in the best position to bargain for the compensation structure you desire. You'll need to know, however, what that prospective employer really thinks of you and how "high" he or she is willing to go. Without that knowledge, you may push too hard—or not hard enough. Since the employer is not likely to confide his or her real feelings to you but may to a third party, an employment counselor can often be of great help during the negotiation stage as a third-party or middleman. Your counselor can also tell the employer about any counteroffers made by your current employer, other job offers you've had, or what you're really worth or will move for—all to help you get the best possible deal.

Create a New Position

One of the best ways to advance a sales career is to create a new position for yourself, either with a present employer or with another firm. It is a project that involves some imagination, research and personal initiative, but the rewards—in terms of career satisfaction and salary—can be great.

Joining a growing company is one excellent way to advance a career. But you may also be able to create a new job for yourself right in your own company. Begin by identifying a need not being met in your office. Suppose you are interested in becoming a sales trainer but your company doesn't offer any formalized sales training. This situation may give you the opportunity to create a position that will advance your own career objectives. You can research the training programs available or even design one yourself. Then it's up to you to sell your company on the idea of sales training —and its benefits for productivity.

Look around other areas of your company. You may be able to make some significant contributions in the area of marketing. For example, your experience in sales can be used to develop sales strategy, produce sales scripts, or improve current sales presentation materials through work with graphic artists. The opportunities are limited only by your energy and initiative.

Another way to decide what new jobs should be created is to follow the systems of established companies. This is especially true for a relatively new or expanding sales force. Many new positions are created as a company expands. Use your imagination in proposing new positions for your department.

Once you have identified your company's needs, do some research. Monitor the amount of work that comes through your office, and analyze how the work is being done. Figure out where the problems are.

Then, write a detailed, but concise proposal explaining the present difficulties, possible solutions, and new positions that should be created to implement the changes. Determine and explain, too, what additional skills and training you might need for a new position.

Make a New Contribution to Your Company

Many companies like to reward employees who make contributions above and beyond the call of duty. This strategy is similar to creating a new position, but it is more narrowly focused. It's success may lead to more responsibility, recognition, and compensation but not necessarily to a promotion or change in title. Look around your department. What bottlenecks or problems are there? What can be improved even if it works okay? Find something, anything, that can be improved. (An item for your checklist in your career journal.) Improve it. Find something else. Improve that too. You will soon develop a reputation for commitment, for getting things done.

There are several ways of generating contribution areas. We've just mentioned problem areas and bottlenecks. To your own list of problem areas add the things you pick up in listening and talking to others. For solutions, talk to others in similar departments or companies who have encountered and shared similar problems. Read trade publications and do some research. Aside from pinpointing problems, you might pinpoint company or departmental objectives. Is there any action you can take to improve systems, facilities or procedures that will bring your company or department closer to their goals? How is it done elsewhere? What can you invent yourself?

Finally, look at other companies both inside and outside of your industry to see how they do things differently. Might some of these things be imported to your company with success?

If you are in the sales department, can you find a way of improving the sales reporting systems or prospect sourcing methods? Would creating a specialty territory by market (type of client) or by product be an asset? Can you think of a modification for the product or service you sell? What about new sales methods, direct mail, brochures or slides?

ADVANCEMENT OPPORTUNITIES WITHIN SALES AND MARKETING

The sales and marketing fields are designed for advancement. Since these fields most directly affect a company's own growth and profitability, most companies encourage the career growth of sales and marketing staff. According to the 1980 biennial **Dartnell Sales Compensation** survey, over half the companies asked stated that they had formal career development programs for sales personnel. The survey asked companies for a list of positions to which sales staff can be promoted. Note that sales positions are often promotable into marketing management. The most representative answers were:

Branch Manager
Sales Manager
General Sales Manager
Senior Sales Rep
Sales Management
Product Management
Major Account Representative
District Manager
Regional Manager
Director of Marketing
District Sales Manager
Nonsales Management
Store Manager
Buyer
Regional Manager
Product Manager
Marketing Manager
Department Manager
Service Manager
Sales Manager
Technical Manager
Marketing Management
District Manager
District Trainer
Vice President of Marketing
Territorial Owner
District Manager
Product Manager
Training Manager
Assistant Division Manager
Division Manager
Assistant Sales Manager
Divisional President
District Sales Manager
Product Manager
Director of Sales
Sales Manager
Station Manager
Regional Manager
Sales Manager
Sales Management
Plant Sales Manager
Assistant Sales Manager
Office Management
Engineering Section Manager
National Account Manager
Senior Account Representative
Product Manager
Field Manager

If you feel adventurous and would like to work for yourself, but do not wish to leave the sales field, you might consider becoming an independent manufacturer's representative. As an independent rep, you will be your own boss and the profits you earn may belong to you. You may be able to select the products (lines) from competing manufacturers that you wish to represent—giving you the best selling advantage. An excellent book on this high-paying sales position is published by the American Management Associations. It's called *How to Get Started as a Manufacturer's Representative* (Krause, AMACOM Executive Books, New York, 1980).

Similarly, in marketing, an individual can advance through all levels, but to advance into some areas may require additional education, such as an MBA.

Below is a partial listing of the upper management positions in marketing that offer advancement opportunities. Each company or industry may have its own variations on this list. Do your own investigation and add to this list. Where do you want to go?

> Advertising Manager
> Brand Manager
> Creative Services Manager
> Director of Corporate Advertising
> Director of Marketing
> Director of Marketing Research
> Director of Marketing Services
> Director of Media and Shows
> Director of Planning and New Products
> Director of Product Development
> Distributor Relations Manager
> Division Marketing Manager
>
> General Marketing Administrator
> Group Brand Manager
>
> International Division Manager
>
> Product Manager
> Public Relations Manager
>
> Regional (Division) Manager
>
> Vice President, Marketing
> Vice President, Merchandizing
> Vice President, Sales and Marketing

If you are just beginning or contemplating a career in either sales or marketing and wish to know more about advancement opportunities, review chapters 3 and 5, on sales and marketing respectively. If you have been in the sales or marketing fields for a while, you should, of course, have a good idea of the opportunities for career advancement within your company or industry. However, you shouldn't be limited by this broad range of opportunities. There are many possibilities connected with sales and marketing that lie just beyond the normal confines of these fields. A discussion of some of the further possibilities follows in the next chapter, "Where Do I Go From Here?"

TELEMARKETING

MARIE T. ROSSI, president of Organized Business Techniques in Valhalla, New York, sells sales training courses to companies in Westchester County. Her expertise is in telephone marketing and she definitely views "telemarketing" as a growth field. "More and more companies are selling and marketing by phone," she says. "And they are selling products/services by phone that have never been sold that way before—such as industrial chemicals. Some companies are literally pulling their sales force in from the field and putting them on the phone."

But, Ms. Rossi, explains, you don't simply "put" someone on the phone. To produce maximum results, a telephone sales force must be carefully trained and effective scripts must be developed for them to use. Usually when a firm hires Ms. Rossi, she will spend a week working with that client to develop a script. While there are standard scripts available, she prefers that input from the client goes into a script. After she works with each client's sales manager or training director to produce a script, she critiques the script and begins to train the client's sales force. Using a script means more than memorization.

"We want them to make the script their own," she says. "So I encourage flexibility. The salesperson must be alert and skilled enough to handle the unexpected. It's important to listen effectively. The script will contain the customer's likely response but the salesperson must be able to proceed smoothly even with a different response."

Ms. Rossi, who scored a big marketing success by selling Aero-Vend Inc., a full-service vending machine company, on the idea of office coffee services with an all-women sales force, believes that sales experience is vital for anyone who plans to train other people. "You shouldn't go into sales training without hands-on experience," she says. "When I began training salespeople, I always tested my ideas in the field first."

Ms. Rossi also founded The Women in Sales Association in 1979 and now serves as chairwoman of the national organization which offers career guidance, professional development through monthly meetings and work sessions, a referral service and other benefits to hundreds of women throughout the nation. She is optimistic about the future of women in sales. "All industries are open to women but you have to have plenty of determination and drive."

For women—or men—interested in entering the lucrative field of industrial sales, she suggests that they concentrate on establishing a track record first. "It's very important to show that you can sell and that you can relate well to other people—your customers and your fellow workers. The best entry route is often through a related field," she notes. "Nurses often do very well in pharmaceutical sales, for example. It's a natural transition. They are used to dealing with doctors, and they are familiar with the medical terminology."

8

Where Do I Go From Here?—Careers Beyond Sales and Marketing

CAREER growth can lead in many rewarding directions beyond the fields of sales and marketing. Sales and marketing are two of the most versatile of career fields. If you've worked in these fields and find that you want something different, you have an excellent experience base to build on. You can cash in on the expertise you have developed and move into something new—without throwing away your career investment, without starting over completely from scratch.

If you wish to switch out of a career in sales or marketing, your major difficulty may be in deciding from among the many different career alternatives. To do this, you must know three things: what talents you have, what kinds of things you would like to do, and what new job will both use your talents and fulfill your desires. To learn these things, begin by reviewing the "Job Finding Primer," especially the initial sections concerning Taking Stock of Yourself, Clarifying Your Objectives, and Identifying Job Possibilities. Then refer to the previous chapter, "Advancing Your Career." After reviewing—and working through—these sections, you should have a good idea of your strengths and interests. Of course, right now there may be reasons why you would like to change careers and there may be things you imagine yourself doing. How do these things compare with the results from the exercises you have worked through in earlier chap-

ters? If there are significant differences you will have to resolve them.

CONSULTING

Consulting is one of the most popular new career directions for people in the sales and marketing areas. If you have an area of expertise, and have recognized credentials, it is likely that you can get others to pay you for it. For many salespeople, especially sales engineers, consulting in purchasing of technical products or services such as computers or telephone systems, can be both lucrative and rewarding. Consulting in this area might involve locating the companies with a need for the product or service, convincing them of the need for consulting, helping to develop systems specifications, contacting vendors and soliciting proposals, evaluating proposals and making recommendations with appropriate price/performance analyses, and supervising the installation of systems.

Salespeople also consult in the management of sales staff and sales programs. They might specialize in the development of complete sales programs from A to Z, or in improving existing sales programs. A particular consultant may specialize in a specific industry or in a specific type of consulting, such as the development of sales compensation programs. A sales consultant might also work in the development of sales presentations and collateral materials.

Another major area of consulting is sales training. Some consultants specialize in the development of customized sales training programs, others in generic selling skills used as brush-ups for existing sales staff or in conjunction with a company's own product-specific training program. In addition, there are many well-established sales training companies in the United States. A sales representative who is interested in the area of sales training may wish to join one of these companies rather than become an independent consultant.

Consulting offers a great many opportunities for people in marketing as well. There are consultants who work in establishing complete in-house marketing programs or who work in evaluating and improving existing ones. On a more narrow focus, marketing consultants work in such areas as: marketing research, sales promotions, direct mail, point-of-purchase displays, advertising, distribution channels, authorized distributor or dealer programs, forecasting, and pricing. In fact, there is no activity performed by professionals working in the marketing field that cannot be the basis for a lucrative and rewarding consulting practice. A step up from consulting in the marketing area is the establishment of a marketing services firm—be it sole-service or specialized in one or more areas.

PRODUCT DISTRIBUTION

Sales representatives who wish to establish their own companies might consider becoming involved in product distribution. You might become a licensed distributor for your company's own product or establish an independent distributorship to handle a variety of product lines from several different companies. Of course, it is not necessary to start your own business to get involved in the field of product distribution. Many sales personnel become involved in the operation and management of distributors and wholesalers. Product brokerage can, similarly, be an alternative route to independence and financial security. In the advertising space sales industry, for example, independent brokerage organizations may represent several magazines and sell space to major advertisers, like luxury automobile manufacturers and liquor and tobacco companies. Independent rep organizations of all types allow the former salesperson to continue selling while controlling his own business and his own profits.

PUBLISHING

Publishing and writing offer unusually wide and often overlooked opportunities. One can, for example, start a trade publication—either one geared to the sales or marketing fields (or to some subsection thereof) or to a particular industry—your industry, whether it be the fast-food industry, franchising or computer-assisted learning systems. *The Nightingale Reports* are a series of tips on sales techniques mailed monthly by subscription to sales departments across the country, containing information useful to sales management and field sales representatives alike. *The Nightingale Reports* offer one model of what can be done. While these reports are generic, it is possible to develop something similar for a specific type of industry. And there are many other kinds of publications that can be started by an enterprising sales or marketing professional who has a flair for prose. In addition to starting a magazine or publication, one can also write for one. A former sales or marketing professional can become a reporter for a business or newsmagazine or paper, or one can write articles for any of the existing trade publications connected with the sales and marketing field. A list of such publications would include the specialized house-organs of professional associations and even your own company's newsletter. More financially rewarding may be to edit such publications, rather than to just write for them; and, in fact, most editors are also charged with reportorial duties as well. If you are interested in writing, you could also consider writing a book. The major drawback to writing as a career is that it is an extremely difficult way to make a living. Most authors combine writing with other income-producing activities. However, if you are a consultant or otherwise in business for yourself, becoming widely published can be a bonus to your business.

TEACHING

The field of education offers additional career opportunities for professionals in the sales and marketing field. Many former sales and marketing professionals combine writing with a career in education. Colleges, graduate schools, community colleges and continuing education programs may offer part- or full-time positions for instructors in business education. It is also not uncommon to find business teachers doubling as consultants, while also publishing in their field of expertise. In fact, one of the most lucrative things to publish can be a textbook.

TRADE SHOW ORGANIZATION

Trade show organization and management offers yet another area for career development. The opportunities in this field include organizing a brand new trade show for an industry in which there are none, or one for an industry in which the existing trade shows leave something to be desired. Trade shows are often sponsored by professional associations, trade publications or independent corporations. There are many positions within existing companies for handling the organization of trade shows. Consulting in how to effectively run a booth at a trade show is another field of expertise. On the other side of the fence are exposition companies which handle the space and support services for trade shows and exhibitions of all kinds.

INDUSTRY ANALYSIS

Finally, sales and marketing professionals who have broad knowledge of their fields can work as industry analysts for financial services companies, like investment or brokerage houses. Industry analysts research and evaluate the future trends for specific industries, companies or products.

ADDITIONAL ALTERNATIVES

Association management may offer rewarding career opportunities for people who have executive abilities and a knack for working with people. The opportunities in this field range from actually starting up a professional association to being an executive member of the association, or to heading up one of its specialized areas, like continuing education, membership management or public relations. Some association workers may be volunteers while others may be paid for full-time career positions.

As discussed in chapter 2, the field of purchasing offers a steady salary and security for sales representatives who want to come in from the cold. Another alternative for both sales and marketing professionals is the field of executive recruiting. Executive recruiters can earn anywhere from $20,000 as trainees to well over $100,000 per year for finding qualified professional sales and marketing personnel for companies.

The foregoing discussion of career alternatives has been designed to provide a representative sampling of the directions you might take. If you are interested in one of these fields, begin researching it by reading and by talking to resource people. Decide what further qualifications or experience you'll need to successfully enter a new field, and develop a career plan by using techniques outlined in chapter 7, "Advancing Your Career."

ADVANCEMENT PROFILE

DEBRA BENTON, better known as D.A., is one saleswoman who has really built on her experience. When she was terminated by a previous employer, she set up her own outplacement company to help firms work with terminated executives. Her company, Benton Management Resources in Denver, Colorado, is now seven years old.

"Being terminated can really knock you for a loop," she says. "I have been able to use my experience to help many firms deal with this problem in a creative and compassionate way."

D.A., who put herself through college selling World Book Encyclopedias—and even won an all-expense paid trip to Europe during spring break in an incentive program—credits her success in sales in part to her mother's influence. "My mother started out selling encyclopedias for World Book and now she has over 200 people working for her," Debra says. "She has won every international selling award there is and she didn't even have a formal education. She really blazed a path for me." Teresa Benton is presently a division manager with Scott-Fetzer, the company that purchased World Book.

Besides heading up her own company, D.A. is founder and executive director of the National Association of Business and Industrial Saleswoman, which currently has about 1,500 members. Since the organization was founded in 1978, D.A. says that the number of women involved in industrial sales has risen from 3% to about 10%. "The fastest-growing industries represent the best opportunities for women," she notes. "High-technology companies, medical, chemical companies—they need people and that means they hire more women. And there's excellent opportunity for growth in these companies. These women often find themselves being groomed for management."

In advising people entering sales careers, D.A. stresses the importance of having a sales job suited to your personality type. "The world is full of different kinds of sales job and some offer more immediate rewards than others," she says. "If you're an impatient person, you're not going to be happy in a job selling expensive computer equipment. In this area, you sometimes have to put in six months just establishing a relationship before you really begin to sell."

FOR FURTHER READING

WHILE there is a wealth of information available concerning the fields of sales and marketing, there is very little available directly concerning job descriptions and career opportunities in these fields. The suggestions for further reading and additional information listed below include sources used by the authors in writing this book. This list is just a partial indication of the many books, directories, periodicals and associations available. (See also the section in chapter 6 entitled "Using Directories, Periodicals, and Reference Books.")

Sales Books and Periodicals

Sales and Marketing Management

Buskirk, Richard H., *Selling: Principles and Practices*. New York: McGraw-Hill, 11th ed., 1982.

Buskirk, Richard H. and Miles, Beverly, *Beating Men at Their Own Game: A Woman's Guide to Successful Selling in Industry*. New York: John Wiley & Sons, Inc., 1980.

Nordstrom, Richard D., *Introduction to Selling*. New York: Macmillan Publishing, 1981.

Pletcher, Barbara, *A Saleswoman's Guide to Career Success*. Homewood, Illinois: Dow Jones-Irwin, 1978.

Riso, Ovid, ed., *Sales Manager's Handbook*, 13th ed., 1980.

Sales Executives Club of New York, *How to Land the Job You Want*. New York: Sales Executives Club, 1980.

Marketing Books and Periodicals

Advertising Age, New York.

Britt, Stewart Henderson, ed., *Marketing Manager's Handbook*, 1973.

Bruell, Victor P. and Heyel, Carl, eds., *Handbook of Modern Marketing*. New York: McGraw-Hill, 1970.

Lipson, Harry A. and Darling, John R., *Introduction to Marketing: An Administrative Approach*. New York: John Wiley & Sons, Inc., 1969.

Mason, Ralph E., et al., *Marketing: Practices and Principles*. New York: Gregg Division, McGraw-Hill, 3rd ed., 1980.

Shapiro, Bernard D., *Sales Program Management*. New York: McGraw-Hill, 1977.

Compensation

Steinbrink, John P., *Compensation of Salesmen*. Chicago: Dartnell Corp., 1982.

Wright, John W., *The American Almanac of Jobs and Salaries*. New York: Avon, 1982.

Purchasing

Diamond, Jay, and Pintel, Gerald, *Retail Buying*. Englewood Cliffs, New Prentice-Hall, 1976.

Dowst, Somerby R., *Basics for Buyers*. Boston: Cahners Publishing Co., 1977.

Heinritz, Stuart F. and Farrell, Paul V., *Purchasing: Principles and Applications*. Englewood Cliffs, New Jersey: Prentice-Hall, 6th ed., 1981.

Purchasing Magazine
Purchasing World

Customer Service

Birsner, E. Patricia and Balsley, Ronald D., *Practical Guide to Customer Service Management and Operations*. New York: Amacom, 1982.

Careers and Advancement

Arnold, Peter and German, Richard, *Bernard Haldane Associates' Job and Career Building*. New York: Harper & Row, 1980.

Association of MBA Executives, *AMBA's MBA Employment Guide*, New York, 1982.

Buchanan, C.B., *How to Get the Right Job in Selling and Marketing*. Garden City: Doubleday & Company, Inc., 1965.

Catalyst Editors, *What to Do With the Rest of Your Life*. New York: Simon & Schuster, 1980.

Chapman, Elwood W., *Scrambling/Zig-Zagging Your Way to the Top*. Los Angeles: J. P. Tarcher, Inc., 1981.

Holbert, Neil, *Careers in Marketing*. Chicago: The American Marketing Association.

Kaye, Beverly L., *Up is Not the Only Way, A Guide for Career Development Practitioners*. Englewood Cliffs, NJ: Prentice-Hall, 1982.

King, David and Levine, Karen, *The Best Way in the World for a Woman to Make Money*. New York: Rawson, Wade, 1979.

Kotter, John P., Fany, Victor A., and McArthur, Charles C.,*Self-Assessment & Career Development*. Englewood Cliffs, New Jersey: Prentice-Hall, Inc., 1978.

Krause, *How to Get Started As a Manufacturer's Representative*. New York: Amacom Executive Books, 1980.

Rogers, Robert S. and Chamberlain III, V.B., *National Account Marketing Handbook*. New York: Amacom, 1981.

Solomon, Marc and Weiner,Norman, *Marketing and Advertising Careers*. New York: Franklin Watts, 1977.

Sperling, JoAnne, *Job Descriptions in Marketing Management*. New York: Amacom, 1969.

Wilinsky, Harriet, *Careers and Opportunities in Retailing*. New York: E.F. Dutton & Co, Inc., 1980.

Directories

Greenbook: International Directory of Marketing Research Houses & Services, New York: American Marketing Association.

International Directory of Market Research Organizations, London, England: Market Research Society.

Magazine Industry Market Place (MIMP), New York: R.R. Bowker.

Marketing Service Organization & Membership Roster, 1981, Chicago: American Marketing Association.

Standard and Poor's Register of Corporations, Directors and Executives, New York: Standard and Poor's.

Standard Directory of Advertising Agencies (The "Red Book"), Skokie, Illinois: National Register Publishing Co, Inc.

Ward's 55,000 Largest U.S. Corporations, Petaluma, California: Ward Publications.

Associations

American Association of Advertising Agencies
666 Third Avenue
New York, NY 10017
212-682-2500

American Marketing Association
250 South Wacker Drive
Chicago, IL 60606
312-648-0536
(New York Chapter: 420 Lexington Ave. New York, NY 212-687-3288)

Association of MBA Executives
305 Madison Avenue
New York, NY 10165
212-682-4490

Association of National Advertisers
155 East 44th Street
New York, NY 10017
212-697-5950

Business & Professional Advertising Association
205 East 42nd Street
New York, NY 10017
212-661-0222

Direct Marketing Association
6 East 43rd Street
New York, NY 10017
212-689-4977

Marketing Research Association
111 East Wacker Drive

Chicago, IL 60601
312-644-6610

National Association of Business and Industrial Saleswomen
90 Corona, Suite 1407
Denver, CO 80218
303-777-7257

National Association for Professional Saleswomen
2088 Morley Way
Sacramento, CA 95825
916-484-1234

Sales Executives Club of New York
114 East 32nd Street
New York, NY 10016
212-661-4610

Sales and Marketing Executives International
330 Lexington Avenue
New York, NY 10168
212-239-1919

Authors' Note

THE *Career Blazers Career Guide for Sales and Marketing* is the product of many months of research and writing, and our aim was to make the work as complete and informative as possible. It was not possible, however, to include everything in the scope of this book and we might have overlooked something you think is important. Your comments, criticisms and suggestions are welcome. Please address them to:

Mr. Hal Cornelius
Vice President
Career Blazers
500 Fifth Avenue
New York, NY 10110

About the Authors

WILLIAM Lewis is president of Career Blazers Personnel Services, Inc. A leader and innovator in the personnel industry, Mr. Lewis is credited with creating the first full-service human resources corporation combining permanent and temporary job services, career consulting and skills training. He is the author of *Resumes For College Graduates*, and the co-author of three other popular books on job-hunting techniques: *Getting A Job In Today's Competitive Market*; *How To Choose, Change, Advance Your Career*; and *The Career Blazers Career Guide For Word Processing*. Mr. Lewis is president of the New York Association of Temporary Services and serves as an independent consultant to personnel firms on an international basis.

Hal Cornelius, senior vice president of Career Blazers, joined the company in 1976 after working on a doctorate in Philosophy at Columbia University. He researched, created and sold the nation's first temporary paralegal service. Mr. Cornelius' sales-related experience includes the development and management of field and telephone sales teams and the creation of a formalized sales training program. In the area of marketing, he has designed and written service brochures, display advertising and direct mail programs. A frequent contributor to the New York Law Journal, Mr. Cornelius is also author of *The Career Blazers Guide For Paralegals* and co-author of *The Career Blazers Career Guide For Word Processing*.